(IT'S ALL GOOD. . .)

by
Michael Humphries

. . . How to achieve

"Peace of Mind" everyday

Read My Life . . .

Read My Story . . .

READ MY BOOK . . .

Dedication

In *Loving Memory* of My Mother

9/11/1924 – 6/14/07

❀

Augustine "Tina" Collier

*I still remember everyday in the evenings when she
would get home from work she would lay down on
the couch to watch TV with me at the other end
as we tickled each others' feet . . . I can still feel
her fingers on my feet, those moments are peaceful
and forever.*

My sister is a breast cancer survivor, my grandfather died of cancer, one of my best friends died of stomach (colon?) cancer at the age of thirty-seven, and my brother is a Regional Vice President for the American Cancer Society. For these reasons, I have made the decision to Donate 10% of the royalties of "It's All Good" to organizations that raise funds for the cure of breast cancer and other cancers as well, in honor of my sister Sherril P. Brandon.

Table of Contents

Introduction

I write this book with confident expectations of changing and/or improving the mind-set and lifestyles of many people. Life has given me so many blessings and awesome experiences. Love, happiness, faith, hope, family, and a lot of unique people have solidified a good life for me. I take none of this for granted, and thank God everyday for my blessed life. I write this book from my heart and soul openly displaying my purpose, accomplishments, the "thrill of victory and the agony of defeat." As I reflect back on my entire life, including its rollercoaster ride of ups and downs, I can shout to the world IT'S ALL GOOD!

My mother passed away about three years ago and as far as I'm concerned, she was the best mother in the world. She was a strong woman of faith, and loved her family so very much. She was always there for me, accepting me for who I am. After she passed away, I looked back and as I reflected on the life she led, it was then I made the decision to write this book. Driven by honest responsibilities, it seemed she was always worrying about something. Later on in my life, I realized I was repeating the same pattern. It became obvious that this excess worry was cheating me of the power to live up to my potential. This "worrying" issue was bringing me down, therefore robbing me of "peace of mind" everyday.

I have a good career and have been exposed to lifestyles of extreme wealth but I don't believe success is just about materialism. I believe the definition of true success is being able to maintain "peace of mind."

Worry was my number one issue but there are so many other issues we must take full control over if we are to have peace each day. Since we can't change yesterday, and tomorrow may never come, it is so important to make sure that we are happy *today*.

As I started to write this book, I began having what I refer to as "mental earthquakes." I set out to show steps necessary to keep worry down to a minimum and found there are so many other distractions that prevent us from living fully. One of the major elements in achieving steady "peace of mind" is total forgiveness. I will share with you the ways I have found to address the many situations in life that possibly can block your happiness, your peace of mind, and prevent you from being the best you can be.

I have come to the conclusion that life is not that complicated but believe there are so many times that we humans make things more difficult than they are. One of my favorite quotes is from Ralph Waldo Emerson: "To be simple is to be great." I hope to show you the simplicity of being happy and living every moment in a state of peace.

This book represents the story of a real person and lessons learned along the way. I keep working everyday to get better at this thing called *life*. My passion is to give hope to so many that have given up, to return joy to people that, due to so many defeats, have lost it along the way. I want to show love to individuals who are now afraid to love and help people reach their dreams and goals. By sharing lessons learned and steps to take, my ultimate message is to make as many people as possible capable of attaining and maintaining the greatest success of all—"Peace of Mind Everyday."

As you read about my life, keep your mind open for some fine tuning in your thought process. I strongly believe it is our choice as to situations of how good things are, or how bad things are. The most recognized motivational man in the industry, Zig Ziglar, says "Success and Happiness are not matters of Chance but Choice." I know we can all learn to be better everyday if it is our desire to do so. If you're content with the way things are and don't have the desire to improve, don't bother to read my book. But chances are if you've gotten to this statement, you're like me, desiring to be a better person.

Journey with me . . .   Read My Life.

Read My Story.

READ MY BOOK

Then hopefully you will say with me
IT"S ALL GOOD . . .

Sunrise

Chapter 1

Sunrise

I was born May 10th, 1954, into a middle class family in Birmingham, Alabama where my first memories extend back before the age of two. Maybe we remember trauma more than other situa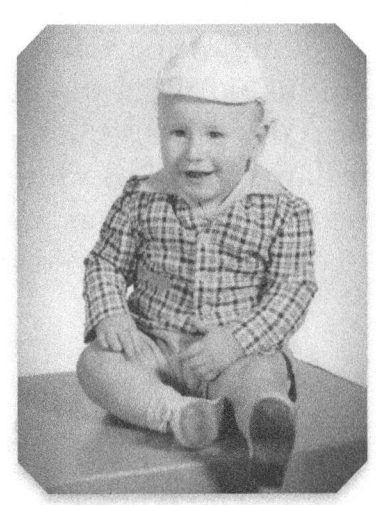tions in our past. I experienced a few events in my early years that classify me as a survivor of misfortunes. Maybe the joy I am capable of feeling now somehow relates to having overcome these misfortunes and appreciating the life I've had.

I remember a scene where I was crawling around on the floor and reaching with my hands to pull myself up. Then my mind goes blank. My sister recently told me that she was there with me at my Aunt Eloise's house, and before anyone could stop me, I put my hands against a gas oven. I still have scars left from second-degree burns on my left palm and third-degree burns on my right palm. At the time the doctors didn't know if I would ever have full use of my hands, but I am thankful that they are both just fine. My next thoughts recall both my hands wrapped in large strips of white gauze. I remember visits to the doctors and how I always began to cry when I realized where I was going.

My mother told me years later that each time the doctor would change the dressings, I would begin to scream. It must have been very painful and my subconscious mind has obviously blocked me from remembering the pain. My mother told me she would always cry with me because it hurt her to see her baby go through such a difficult experience.

As I got older I would have temper tantrums any time I heard anyone mention a visit to the doctor. My parents would always try and keep it a secret but I had sharp ears. I was a sickly child with throat problems and a vulnerability to colds. There were many trips to the doctor and I remember being chased all over the house. But the grown ups always won and I would end up in the car headed toward the doctor's office. To be honest with you, I am still apprehensive when I have to see a doctor.

Every Summer we would take our annual vacation. My father only got one week each year for a vacation. It was always a small family reunion because my mother's sister, Eloise, and her family, would always meet us in Panama City, Florida. On occasions my grandparents would meet us there. We always rented the same house, two blocks from the beach. Lucy Mae, our housekeeper and baby-sitter, would go with us. I remember all the grilling of barbeque, hamburgers, and hot-dogs. My cousin Terry was about my age. He and I would run up and down the beach and play in the waves. One of my favorite things was playing putt-putt at a small theme park across the street from the beach. The beach-es on the pan-handle of Florida are extremely beautiful, with its pure white sand as white as snow. I believe it was during this early stage of my life that I fell in love with the ocean.

I remember two specific instances as a kid that landed me in trouble. I'm sure there were many but these are the two that stand out in my memory. I was always told never to get into a car unless an adult I already knew was putting me there. Hueytown's' claim to fame was its two race car drivers, The Allison Brothers. One day I found one of the doors unlocked in my mother's 1957 Chevrolet and decided to get behind the wheel and pretend to be driving like Bobby or Donny Allison. The next thing I knew my grandmother was yanking me out, and spanking my little rear end.

The other incident that stands out is one of me and one of my little girl friends pulling down our pants as we ran down the driveway singing how we were Mr. and Mrs. Butt. My grandmother happened to be looking out the window. I don't know how she was so fast but when we got to the bottom of the driveway, there she was. Again, I got Mr. Butt's rear end worn out pretty badly. This said, please know that I loved my grandmother very much and can honestly say IT'S ALL GOOD.

I also remember many visits to see my father in the hospital and he was always in a wheel chair. I was too young to go up to his room, so my mother would always bring him outside to see me. I didn't know for quite some time why he was in a wheelchair or in the hospital. My father had worked several years for Pullman Steele Manufacturing. He had a good job and was able to support his family providing a nice house, new car and all the things we needed until he was injured.

One thing I remember about the hospital visits was every time a nurse or anyone wearing a white uniform passed by, I would start crying and jump in his or my mother's arms. They assured me these people would not hurt me. As time went on, they realized it was not the people but the uniforms that scared me. Those uniforms were taking me back to the rooms where the dressings on my hands were changed and all the doctors, nurses, and medical staff surrounded me.

The day that stands out most as a child was May 6, 1960. I was at my grandmother's house on a Saturday afternoon about ten miles from our home in Hueytown. My mother came by to pick me up, and my older brother Ron was with her. She received a phone call and told my brother and I to rush and get in the car. She took off, peeled down the road as if we were in a drag race. I remember asking her to please slow down because I had never been in a car going so fast and it was frightening. But she kept assuring me that everything was ok. I think we were about halfway to our house when we passed a phone booth and my mother slammed on the breaks to make a call. Obviously, no one had cell phones back then. When she got back in the car with a stricken face, she told my brother there was no answer. We flew into our driveway coming to a screeching stop. My brother jumped out and ran toward the front door, my mother making an effort to stop him. But he got past her, so she picked me up and her tears were soaking into my shoulder. Within seconds my brother came running out screaming *Oh My God, Oh My God.* I didn't know what was going on but I remember I felt terrified by the expression on his face. Suddenly our next door neighbors were there and my mother told me everything was okay, to go and see a movie with my friend James who lived next door. As I write this, with tears running down my face, keep in mind I was only seven years old and couldn't grasp what was happening, what had actually happened.

The following day in my mother's arms, I saw my father's body lying in a casket in our living room. The house was full of people. I have no immediate memories other than those details. I found out later that the phone call my mother received at my grandmother's was from my father, telling her he "couldn't take it anymore," and was going to take a shot gun and kill himself. When my mother stopped at the pay phone and got no answer, she assumed he had followed through with his desperation. He had called to tell her one last time he loved her and to take good care of us.

My father had been in a wheelchair since he was laid off at his job and decided to go in with some of the other men who lost their jobs and make illegal alcohol in the mountains. One night the steal factory where they were brewing the alcohol was raided and as all the men ran off in different directions, my father took three shots in his back, one of which hit him directly in the spine.

My father was, no doubt, stripped of his dignity. He had been the breadwinner supporting his family with a comfortable life-style. And there was also the issue of pain. A doctor would come to our house almost every day to give him morphine shots.

I don't, in any way at all, justify my father taking his own life. I believe life is the most precious gift of all and we should never lose respect for that gift. But neither will I ever judge him for  what he did. That was fifty years ago and I can't imagine the situation or his mindset. All I can do is forgive him, and I have.

Forgiveness is an important part of my message, but I will state here that forgiving someone doesn't mean you agree with everything that person has done. Forgiving doesn't make you forget. Even though you don't condone what a person has done, you must choose to forgive completely in order to abolish future pain that might keep you from being able to choose every day to be happy and have "Peace of Mind." If you are critical of others, judging them by your own personal standards, you will never achieve true "Peace of Mind." In general, if we would spend more time counting our blessings rather than judging others, the world be a much better place.

Please God . . . please

. . . Grant me the serenity

to accept the things I cannot change;

courage to change the things I can;

and wisdom to know the difference.

Living one day at a time;

Enjoying one moment at a time;

Accepting hardships as the pathway to peace;

Taking, as He did, this sinful world

as it is, not as I would have it;

Trusting that He will make all things right

if I surrender to His Will;

That I may be reasonably happy in this life

and supremely happy with Him

Forever in the next.

Amen.

Of course, with my Father gone, my Mother had to work full time to support the family. To do so, she worked in a meat processing plant. At her job she was required to wear a white uniform. I remember many evenings my Mother pulling into the driveway as she arrived home from work. I would usually be out in the front yard playing because I knew about what time to expect her. But every time she got out of the car I would run and hide. She thought I was playing a game and would go inside to take a shower to get cleaned up before making dinner. I would always be waiting for her in the living room to run and jump into her arms.

One day I was inside when she came home and as soon as I saw her I started crying, saying that I was afraid of her. She kept her distance and asked why I was afraid. I cried out, "it's your dress, it scares me." To be precise, it was actually the uniform she was wearing that I associated with all the medical uniforms from my past. Once she understood the situation, she always took a change of clothes with her to work, so that I never saw the uniform again.

Even as a kid I was a little eccentric. When all the other kids would sit on the ground and play, I would only lean over, wanting to remain squeaky-clean. Despite that, I had an appetite for eating the dirt, which was Alabama red clay. The doctor told my mother, however, to let me eat all the dirt I wanted because it was loaded with rich minerals.

It's strange how we recall the details of certain traumas in our childhood. I'm sure the imprint of those white uniforms was heavily formed in my memory. Still, all my early memories are not about being frightened. One of my fondest memories of my Mother was that once she had settled in from work, she would lay at one end of the couch with me at the opposite end and we would tickle each others' feet while watching TV. I can still feel the touch of my Mother's hands on my feet. I would feel so bonded with her at those times. Thank you Mother for tickling my feet and showing me every day how much you loved me.

Sweet Home Louisiana

Chapter 2

Sweet Home Louisiana

A couple of years after my father died my Mother remarried to a man named Joe Collier. Joe was the foreman of the plant my Mother worked in and he had lost his wife to cancer before my father died. My Dad knew Joe and Dad told my mother that if anything ever happened to him, she should marry Joe. He said that Joe was a good man, that he would make a good husband and good father to his children.

A couple of years after my father was gone, he got his wish. Joe became my new dad and time would prove I had one of the best dads ever. He was very quiet, or maybe it was that back then my Mother wouldn't let him get a word in edgewise. Did I mention that my mother loved to talk? I believe I may have inherited that trait.

Joe had a kind heart, integrity, a lot of love to share and everyone liked him. He had a dry sense of humor and most people appreciated him for who he was. My father was right; Joe was one of the best fathers and an awesome husband to my mother.

Joe had three children from his first marriage so at the beginning we had a full house, an earlier version of "The Brady Bunch." I believe it was about a year after my mother and Joe married that Joe took a job in Roanoke, Alabama, about two hours east of Birmingham. At that time, Roanoke was a small town; the population was only about five thousand. We first lived in a town called Rock Mills, five miles from Roanoke. Rock Mills held the county's water supply and had waterfalls about two blocks from us. We had some really great times walking across the falls and playing in the water.

I realize now that as kids, we sometimes don't appreciate some of the things we did the way we do as we get older. We lived in this sixty-year old home that had been built for the manager of the water supply source. With its screened-in porch wrapped all the way around the 2500 foot perimeter of the house, it was an amazing piece of property. It had wide, plank, hardwood floors throughout, and when you looked outside the back door the view was that of a hilly field with huge earth-toned rocks everywhere and a refreshing creek running through it. Cows browsed there as well. For me to have a place like that now would be quite the ticket!

Before we left Birmingham, my brother Bobbie was born. It seemed like a lot kids married younger then because it wasn't long before the only ones left were myself and two other brothers. Bobbie, Bill and myself, along with Mother and Joe, made up the Collier-Humphries household.

In Roanoke I remember going to my first campaign rally downtown. Big Jim Folsom was a former governor running for the office again. I really don't recall much about him but I can still see him introducing Hank Williams' widow and her son Hank, Jr. who was about my age. I was familiar with Hank Williams Sr.'s music because my Mother used to play it a lot at home. She used to clean the house with "I'm So Lonesome I could Cry" or "Your Cheatin' Heart" blaring in the background. And then there was a song I always found amusing, titled "There's a Tear in Beer . . . "

A couple of years went by and Joe was offered a position in Alexandria, LA; I was about ten at the time. Alexandria was located in central Louisiana about 180 miles northwest of New Orleans. I guess it was a pretty good offer because the next thing I knew we were on our way to Louisiana. I was in the fifth grade when we moved to our new city and my mother enrolled me in Rug Elementary School.

I believe children adapt to change faster then most adults because I felt right at home.

On the other hand my Mother was not so happy. It was hard for her to uproot herself and her family after spending most of her life within miles from where she was born. But as time went by, as we celebrated holidays and got used to the new town with its larger population and new mall, within a year, she was telling everyone it felt like home.

Our house in the country lay across the road from the meat processing plant. There was a bayou with cypress trees that ran behind the plant, and the house itself was surrounded by acres of cotton fields. It was a fun place to live with wildlife and tropical birds everywhere. One night when we pulled in there was a wild cougar in the driveway. I was so afraid, it took me thirty minutes to get out of the car.

And of all things in the world to make her really happy, she loved The Piccadilly Cafeteria. My mother started selling Avon products and in a short time it seemed like we were living in an Avon factory because Avon lipsticks, creams and ladies' compacts were everywhere. She was a smashing success;

she wouldn't stop talking to a customer until they bought something.

Eventually Joe quit his job and went into the insurance business. He did very well with insurance and was promoted to state director of the company. My mother got her licenses and started selling insurance as well. They both became very good in their new industry, and looking back, I admire them for stepping out of their comfort zone of security to make a better life for themselves and their family.

Before we moved from Alabama I had begun to listen to and sing gospel music. I soon realized I loved singing and as time kept ticking by my vocal skills developed. I remember before we left Birmingham I had my first opportunity to sing in public at Hopewell Baptist Church which was my grandparents' church. The pastor put a chair behind the pulpit so people could see me and I stood on the chair and sang "I'll Fly Away" with passion and enthusiasm.

In Alexandria I started singing at any church that would have me and the more I sang, the more I improved. I could feel my pitch hitting the notes perfectly and my voice soaring better and better. Soon my family became active members of Hope Missionary Baptist Church. I sang at our home church on a regular basis, sang at community events, on some of the local television shows, and at the age of twelve recorded my first solo album. I also met the gospel group Twin City Quartet, and started traveling with them on the weekends selling my records.

By the age of fourteen, I was promoting concerts bringing top names in Southern gospel music from talent agencies out of Nashville. Just before promoting my first concert, I went to see Joel and Labreeska Hemphill perform at a small Pentecostal

JIMMIE DAVIS
Box 2626
Baton Rouge, La.

church where I had sung many times. The pastor of the church, Sister Ora Youngblood, was so nice to me, allowing me to sing any time I wanted. The Hemphills were just getting their start. Joel pastored at a church in Bastrop, Louisiana and even though I was just a kid, he took a lot of time talking to me after the concert. Thank you Joel, for your kindness, IT'S ALL GOOD.

* * *

For my first promotion I booked the Hemphills, the Twin City Quartet and, of course, myself. I rented the Alexandria Convention Center, which seated about fourteen hundred people. I think we only sold about sixty tickets, maybe enough to pay one group. There was the cost of the convention center, advertising and performers. My first effort as a producer was a total loss.

I was a little discouraged but loved singing so much and was not going to let this loss stop me. Other than selling my little records,

I developed another source of income. I walked the sidewalks of Alexandria picking up pecans, then I sold them for twenty-five cents a pound.

The profits of thousands of pecans and records sold continued to back my concert promotions. And I kept promoting despite losing money. One of the people I met and was able to perform with several times was Governor Jimmy Davis. He was a two-term governor of Louisiana and wrote the classic song "You Are My Sunshine." The first time I met him I had the same experience as when I met Joel Hemphill. Governor Davis went out of his way to encourage and motivate me.

Governor Davis was inducted into the Country Music Hall of Fame, has several state parks named in his honor, and built the Sunshine Bridge crossing over the Mississippi River. I loved politics, government, and gospel music, which made the experience of knowing him one of the most treasured of my life up to that point. For me his greatest legacy was being kind and encouraging to a fifteen year-old kid. Governor Davis passed away November 5, 2000. Thank you, Governor Davis, for your contribution to my life. You are one of the reasons I can say to everyone IT'S ALL GOOD.

Certain quotations I've read apply to him. Wilfred Grenfell said "The service we render others is the rent we pay for our room on earth." And although I think of him as wise, more often I think of him as kind; therefore Jean-Jacques Rousseau's words also bring him to mind. "What wisdom can you find that is greater than Kindness." My own words bring him to mind as well as many of my other supporters: "A kind heart; A gentle heart, will return kind, gentle blessings, to enhance your purpose and dreams."

Yours truly—Michael Humphries.

But Governor Jimmy Davis' lyrics will ring eternally in our minds . . . "You are my sunshine, My only sunshine. You make me happy when skies are gray." –

* * *

As I continued to promote concerts, after a while they started to pay off. I then began breaking even and eventually made a little money on them. This taught me at an early age that passion and persistence pay off.

During this period our town of Alexandria was growing and built a new high school. When I went into a high school as a freshman the school had just opened. It was awesome having a school that was brand new. The building was in a cow pasture but it was a shiny new, impressive structure and most importantly, beginning high school, excited about extracurricular activities and finding a group to sing with.

Since I had fractured my back playing football a couple of years earlier, I had no interest in playing sports, only music. I tried out for the first Alexandria Sr. High Choir and, with my singing experience, was a shoe-in. My next step was to join The Alexandrians, directed by Charles G. Crump. This was the chorale seeking only *the best* and I was the only freshman to make the cut. The only down side to being the lone freshman singer meant after my freshman year was finished, many of my best friends graduated because they were seniors. Still, the second year was fun and productive because The Alexandrians were a close-knit group.

But my personal focus was still on gospel music. I kept dreaming of being on the road, singing full time with a professional group. I started sending my records to groups all over the country. The Hemphills moved to Nashville and became one of the biggest names in gospel music. I stayed in touch with all the connections I had made through the concert promotions.

Again, thanks to my persistence, a letter came in the mail one day from The Journeymen based out of Boston, MA. I had just finished my sophomore year and my Mother was not ready to let her baby go to another corner of the country and be left to the care of total strangers.

Steve Sanders, a soloist who was my age, performed with The Florida Boys and later in life he became the baritone singer for the

Oakridge Boys. One night during a concert where the Florida Boys were introducing Steve Sanders, I found him outside sitting in the bus and banged on the window. When I got Steve's attention, after telling him how much I loved his music from The Gospel Singing Jubillee Show on television, I asked how he was managing to attend high school while traveling and performing. He told me about a school in Chicago. Later, without my mother knowing, I applied and was accepted into The American School in Chicago to finish my high school education through correspondence. It was quite a challenge convincing my mother, but finally after enough pouting, begging and my mother's tough conversations with the owner of the group, she finally gave in.

Off to Boston I flew with amazing experiences about to come into my life. I was determined not to give up my dream. I kept on keeping on and wouldn't allow anyone or anything to stand in the way of the future I was creating for myself.

In achieving your dreams, persistence is more important than talent, IQ, or education.

I do not underestimate these qualities in a person. I just believe that with true passion and belief in that passion, anything is attainable. My sixth grade teacher Walter B. Gatlin ran for police juryman in a district of Rapids Parish, LA. I was interested in politics and asked him if I could help in any way. He gave me his brochure with all his qualifications and his appeal for people's votes, and on the back was a poem that has inspired me for the rest of my life. This poem is something I look at everyday.

Don't Quit

When things go wrong, as they sometimes will,

When the road you're trudging seems all up hill,

When the funds are low and the debts are high,

And you want to smile, but you have to sigh,

When care is pressing you down a bit.

Rest if you must; but don't you quit.

Life is queer with its twists and turns,

As everyone of us sometimes learns,

And many a failure turns about

When he might have won had he stuck it out;

Don't give up, though the pace seems slow;

You might succeed with another blow.

Often the goal is nearer than

It seems to a faint and faltering man.

often the struggler has given up

When he might have captured the victor's cup.

And he learned too late, when the night slipped down,

How close he was to the golden crown.

Success is failure turned inside out;

The silver tint of the clouds of doubt;

And you never can tell how close you are,

It may be near when it seems afar;

So stick to the fight when you're hardest hit—

It's when things seem worst than you must not quit.

—Anonymous

Chapter 3

Gospel Music is The Thing

I had never been to New England before; as a matter of fact, Tennessee was the furthest north I'd ever traveled. I had already started my correspondence classes with The American School and the negotiation process with my Mother and the Journeymen group took a little time.

I flew into Logan Airport on the cold winds of January. When I stepped off the plane, a stranger to the regional temperatures, I felt like I was in Alaska. Soon enough however, I was settled into my new apartment furnished by the group. I'll never forget those first few

(Journeymen)

days. I felt like I had moved into a cold foreign country populated with people that spoke English but with accents so heavy, at times I had a hard time understanding some of their words. I guess this was my first experience with English as a Second Language! I was reminded of The Wizard of Oz:" *Dorothy, You're not in Kansas anymore.*

Still, it didn't take me long before I was speaking Yankee with the best of them. I had always been outgoing and able to entertain people in various surroundings. I realized that these New Englanders loved my southern accent and I used it to my advantage. Don Pearsson was the owner, baritone and manager of The Journeymen and he always M.C.ed the concerts and during each program he would always turn the microphone over to me three or four times. He wanted everyone to hear my Southern accent, so I'd refer to the crowd as "so many nice Yankees" and drawl my way into entertaining everyone especially with the song "O What a Happy Day."

The Journeymen group consisted of Tom Perrson, Joe Van Huis, Dana Kirkpatrick, and of course, myself, singing lead.

* * *

I was blessed in meeting some of the most amazing people of my lifetime after living in New England for just a short time. We performed at The Wareham United Methodist Church about fifty miles south of Boston, a small community at the top of Cape Cod. It was a place that made me feel at home. Grace was the pianist for the church where I met so many kind and friendly parishioners. They absolutely raved about The Journeymen. Upon our second visit, it was as though some of these people were treating me like family. I was overwhelmed with the pretty girls who latched onto me. Several girls I went out with went on to beauty queens later. Wonderful, magical things started happening as a result of these people in Wareham. That was nothing compared to meeting and becoming a part of the Perry Family. The family consisted of Mom and Dad Perry along with thirteen children. The oldest was Grace and the youngest one was Tom. Grace had never married and treated me like a son. She was such an incredible human being. Her life was devoted to giving and sharing with others her creative gifts and her faith. A talented vocalist and pianist, it was her character that separated her from everyone else. I had my Mother in Louisiana and I had Grace while on the road so I was covered on both ends. And my Mother and Grace became the best of friends. These two women are so much a part of who I am today. I was as close to Grace as a friend as is humanly possible.

Dad Perry had built the house right around the corner from the church for his new bride as they were preparing for the birth of their first daughter, Grace. An unpaved road led up to the tiny wood-shingled cape house that sat amongst five acres of forest land. They kept building onto the house as the thirteen children were born. Everyone shared and a bed and I slept in the unheated attic with a few of the kids. Grace always made sure she turned on the space heater in the bathroom if I was going to take a shower. I was a picky eater too and Grace would always cook me a separate meal when I didn't like Mom Perry's dinners. When we walked on the beach, I was always shocked when Grace opened mussels and ate them raw. It became a joke between us as she kept suggesting I try one too. We also played an ESP card game guessing which card the other was holding. We got to the point with our synchronous energy that we could guess correctly about 90% of the time.

Grace was truly a fascinating woman. As editor of the Wareham Journal, Grace published several articles on ESP and Aliens. She documented cases of public sightings of UFOs. One night driving in New Hampshire or Vermont, she told us to focus on the belief in UFOs. She made me a believer because I knew she'd never lie to me. As we all focused, we asked for a sign and suddenly something, a huge energy like a live football stadium, swooped down and over us. I couldn't believe what I was seeing. We tried over and over several times after that, but were never successful in manifesting such a strange miracle again.

I was with the Journeymen for a little less than a year. Just before the group was getting ready to take a West Coast tour I decided to quit the group. Things were not going the way I expected and I decided to form my own group. For one thing I felt our means of transportation, a gutted out bread truck, was hard for me to drive. We didn't have a hired driver like Nashville groups and I began resenting having to drive the truck in the mountains and in the snow. I was honestly scared I would have an accident and kill us all. This became a huge issue. The schedule was also grueling and I wasn't making as much money as I did part-time when I was in Louisiana. Another reason I left was because I felt I wanted my own group.

Mike Humphries and the Anchors made up the second full time group for me to perform with. I was an eighteen-year old kid living heaven on earth. Grace and Tom joined my group after the West Coast tour was over.

We would spend about half the year working out of Wareham and the other half from Alexandria. Platus, a comedian at the time

(The Anchors)

of the Roman Republic, said "Your wealth is where your friends are." And the Roman philosopher Cicero said "Man's best support is a very dear friend." But the famous French diarist, Anais Nin, put it this way, " Each friend represents a world in us, a world possibly not born until they arrive and it is only by this meeting that a new world is born." I felt I had found this new world.

One of the songs I recorded, "I Found A Better Way," was written by Joel Hemphill. As I review my life and all the incredible experiences in gospel music and life after gospel music, I can honestly say I continue in life to find a better way. I learned as a seventeen year old what it was to be responsible, manage a group, pay for recording sessions, show up on time and do what was expected of me. Moving north to Massachusetts opened my mind to integrated churches, integrated marriages. My Southern background and Pentecostal youth was less structured than the liberal minded people up north. People up north weren't necessarily cold, but their service was more structured. They just didn't show as much emotion as people did in the South. When I look back I was learning lessons about responsibility and my mind was opening. For people that want to be happy and help others to be happy, I think we keep growing everyday as long as we desire to grow. Desiring to grow requires an open mind to other people's needs, belief systems, and desires. We need to respect everyone for who and what they are. You should never get to the point of believing you are right and everyone else is wrong. We all need to have the desire to learn something new everyday and live "one day at a time." I learned this as young teenager.

* * *

At the age of twenty-two I fell in love with my Pastor's daughter Deborah, and we were married in 1976. Spending time back in Alexandria gave me the opportunity to become a member and get very involved in the fastest growing southern Baptist Church in Louisiana. I was constantly juggling my schedule around singing and other church activities since I was The Youth Director of my church. One thing I enjoyed so much about gospel music was traveling and seeing all the different regions of the country. I think we live in a beautiful, diverse country. Each region has something special to offer. I now live in South Florida and I adore the tropical climate, plants and skies. Being born and raised in the South, well, there's something to be said for Southern hospitality. As far as scenery and views, I am partial to upper New York state and Northern New England. For me these landscapes are breathtaking. Mountains were new to me and I found the views from up high to be gorgeous. I was also introduced to the colors of autumn and the fall became my favorite season.

In my new group we traveled in a dual cab Ford pickup pulling a trailer that could sleep ten people and store our equipment. While traveling through Vermont one day I saw a large, snow-covered field with mountains in the background. I asked the driver to pull over. As I started running across the fresh white powder of the snow I leaped about twenty yards and instantly dropped into the snow up to my face!

At first my life flashed in front of me because I thought I was going to keep going down but then my feet hit a solid surface and I started laughing uncontrollably. Everyone else was watching from the side of the road and started laughing with me. I have a tendency to laugh without being able to stop when something scares me. Someone in the group walked slowly out to me to pull me out. My laughing was contagious and soon laughter rippled through the entire group. A couple of guys were walking along the side of the road and saw what happened. They said I was really lucky I hadn't drowned because underneath that snow was a large lake where they fished but it never froze over for winter fishing. The thing that kept me from drowning was a thin layer of ice.

On another trip thorough Vermont in the spring on this winding road someone screamed, "Look at the ground hog!" Looking out of the window, I saw my first ground hog in a green field. Up till then I didn't know a groundhog from a skunk. I always thought groundhogs were mythic. They are strange looking little creatures because they were four-legged animals, but they run on two legs.

Another experience that I'll never forget was just outside Meriden, MS. The group was on a tour and staying overnight in a cabin that belonged to someone's distant relatives. I was taking a shower and saw a shadowy thing coming out of the drain. At first I thought is was a worm but then realized it was the tongue of a snake. I've always been scared of snakes and jumped out of the shower butt naked, running out of the bathroom screaming about snakes in the bathtub. Grace threw me a blanket to cover myself. The group was used to me playing jokes and I thought this was one of them. (One of my jokes was to scare everyone by opening the driver's door, honking the horn and screaming.) Grace and Tom followed me back into the bathroom where we viewed a five-foot rattle snake in the tub. Needless to say no one else would take a shower there.

I could go on and on about how I was impressed by so many sites, scenes and sounds Mother Earth offers us each day. There is so much to love. Enjoy these blessings everyday—snakes, groundhogs, snow showers, mountains–they don't cost a dime. Don't take them for granted. Everyday I see sights that amaze me. Most of the time they are images of one of God's creations, trees, birds, flowers. Life is amazing and yet can be very simple. Why do we as humans want to complicate matters? IT'S ALL GOOD to simply accept and enjoy the natural world. Simplicity is one of the best things in life.

Shortly after that I disbanded my group and took a job singing baritone with The Southmen from Gadsden, Alabama. It was another new beginning, and yet the sad thing was that I would never see Grace again. She passed away several years ago in her sleep. IT'S ALL GOOD for I now have another angel watching over me.

Chapter Four

Dreams of a Twelve Year Old

Gadsden, Al. is a small town about 100 miles north of Birmingham, Alabama, my birth place. This was home to The Southmen. The group, owned by Jim Hefner, was going through a reorganization phase when we first met. Jim and his wife Julie had a basement apartment that my wife and I moved into. Julie was a Southern belle, beautiful with a gentle sweet spirit. I loved her long brown hair and her natural look. She was so kind to us. She was always making sure we had everything we needed, popping in frequently to check on us and make us feel at home. During this time Julie became a good

SOUTHMEN

P.O. Box 1618
Gadsden, AL 35902
(205) 547-2673

(Southmen)

friend to me. She shared stories of her family which helped me to open up about my stories and we became very close by that sharing. She believed in me and that the group would be very successful.

Julie lost a battle with cancer a few years ago. Jim told me after she passed away that she loved me in a special way. Although it was tough on her and everyone who loved her, heaven and I gained another angel and this is why I say IT'S ALL GOOD . . .

* * *

The Southmen were in the main stream of southern gospel music and to be smack in the middle of that scene was what I had always dreamed of. Jim sang tenor and was also the M.C. He had a reputation in gospel music as being one of the funniest people in the industry. His very dry sense of humor made crowds roar in laughter. He was as funny off stage as well as on stage. Traveling with him was quite an entertaining experience. This man made me laugh to the point of tears often in times of difficulty.

One time we were checking out of a motel in Georgia while a couple was checking in. They had left their luggage outside the office. Jim nonchalantly picked up their luggage and just carried it around the corner of the building and left it there. Getting into the bus we were all laughing till our sides hurt imagining the expression on the couple's faces when they think that their luggage was stolen.

Another time, after giving a concert, as we were leaving a hospitable visit for dinner with the pastor and his wife, Jim popped into the mudroom on the way out. Inside there must have been twenty-five bags of pecans. Again, casually Jim grabbed a bag and took it with him. We couldn't believe he did this right in front of our hosts but they never noticed. Thank you Jim for all the humor and laughs. I learned a good lesson working with him. Sometimes when you're backed up against the wall, humor is the best medicine and most of us know IT'S ALL GOOD . . . when you laugh.

Buddy Burton was our lead singer and I believe to this day he was one of the best vocalists in gospel music. Buddy and I had our own unique friendship. With Buddy I could talk about anything. We were able to have real heart-to-heart talks about the things that matter in life. We had detailed conversations about our belief systems, sharing the tough things we'd been through and the issues we were experiencing right at the time. He later sang lead for The Gold City Quartet, which is one of the biggest name groups in southern gospel music.

As we traveled the country, making more and more of a name for ourselves, things started really shaping up for us. We had fans that would drive 200 miles to hear us sing on a Saturday night. Many of these fans were women. Maryann Price lived in Birmingham where we often stayed. She did more for the band than anyone else, putting us up at her house, feeding us and sharing her positive energy. Thank you Maryann Price for your hospitality and good cooking. Performing at major concerts across the country almost every weekend, the Southmen were headed for the top of the gospel movement.

Since my interest in the music business kept expanding, as I continued singing with the Southmen, my wife and I decided to move to Nashville. Deborah was excited about relocating not only because she liked the idea of a big city, moreover, she liked country music and, of course, Nashville was Music City, Home of the Grand Ole Opry.

The biggest promoter in gospel music at the time, however, was J.G. Whitfield, the original manager and baritone singer of the Dixie Echoes Quartet from Pensacola, Florida. Mr. Whitfield left The Dixie Echoes to be a Gospel Music Promoter. I knew of him since I'd been ten or eleven years old. Jim Hefner knew Mr. Whitfield. Shortly after I began singing with The Southmen, he started booking us with other big name gospel groups almost every weekend. I had a lot of respect for this man because I had known of him as a kid. He himself was a legend in gospel music industry. I told him how long I'd followed him and what an honor it was to meet him. Everyone in gospel read his monthly publication *The Singing News*. He had a mustache like Charlie Chaplin and in my mind was almost as famous.

One of the biggest compliments we received was after one of the concerts when Mr. Whitfield told Jim and I that we were one of the best selling groups in gospel music, and that we had a way of exciting a crowd unlike any other group. Thank you Mr. Whitfield. I can still see you on stage introducing us to a roaring audience. IT'S ALL GOOD . . . It was an honor and privilege to know you.

One night while performing at an outdoor venue in western Georgia, somehow we moved to our next plateau. This happened at a music theme park built to bring in the top names of country music three times a month and it was our first time there. It had a stage about five feet high, a roof and about 4000 seats. My older brother Ron and his wife

Linda had come over from LaGrange to see us perform. The group was polished by this time and we were going in the right direction. We just needed a little kick to push us a little higher.

While singing, the Holy Spirit took over, and before I knew it I had jumped off the stage and was dancing in the sawdust. The full house of three thousand went crazy. We had a hard time getting off the stage that night because our fans didn't want us to stop. My lesson that night was to learn I should never hold back; when you're seized by the spirit of your own passion, don't be afraid to move with it. When you allow your passion to show it goes viral and everyone else is also seized with enthusiasm. IT'S ALL GOOD . . . One definition of passion is "boundless enthusiasm." Risk showing your passion from time to time.

We sang at the National Quartet Convention in Nashville shortly after that performance. This allowed me to see a lot of people I hadn't seen in a while, groups I had worked with over the years. It was a huge reunion. The biggest event of the night was when Elvis made a surprise visit and sang three or four songs. A few weeks later J.G. Whitfield booked us for the 1979 Singing News Convention in Birmingham, a two day event, and Mr. Whitfield booked only his favorite groups, The Goodmans, J.D. Sumner and The Stamps Quartets, Jerry Goff and the Singing Goffs. We made Mr. Whitfield proud. We got a standing ovation when we went on stage and once we started to perform the place was on fire. I remembered that kid with dreams of arriving at this notorious concert someday.

IT'S ALL GOOD.

Thank you gospel music for all the people and experiences brought into my life. Gospel music will always be a part of me and for this reason I went back into the studios for the first time in more than 30 years to record a new inspirational c d. YouTube: mhitsallgood (channel).

Chapter 5

A Heart Stops Beating

The weekend after that landmark concert we 'd planned on taking off for some badly needed rest. I was spending that week at home in Nashville with my wife and some time in recording studios as well. Jerry Goff, one of gospel music's finest groups, had a couple of guys quit and called me to ask if I might be able to fill in for concerts he had booked that weekend. I decided to help him out and had a great time singing with him. He was a class act. I'll never forget how the weekend ended up. Jerry was booked for an outdoor event in rural Pennsylvania on Sunday afternoon. Thousands of fans from all over the northeast had traveled to be there. It was quite an experience performing for all these people with beautiful mountains in the background. It felt like something about the mountains majestically held us in their lap. Jerry was headed in another direction from there, so I hitched a ride back to Nashville on one of the other groups' buses since I had to sing with the Southmen the following week. IT'S ALL GOOD . . . when you're singing gospel with Jerry Goff looking at a massive crowd, with God's own mountains overhead.

My wife was pregnant at the time and I felt guilty when I would leave her, hitting the road for days at a time. But I kept singing as proposals were coming in from other groups offering more money, though I was starting to get restless and didn't feel the time was right to start over with another group. Even though I was living out my dream looking at a bright future in gospel music, my passion was beginning to fade. I believe that sometimes when you have a goal or a dream, that it's the process of getting there, the journey, that is the best part.

A few weeks after the trip to Pennsylvania, we had planned a full weekend in and around Birmingham. I asked my wife, who was in her eighth month, if she would like to go with me. She said "absolutely" because it had been a while since she had heard The Southman sing. After all the concerts as we drove back to Nashville late Sunday afternoon, Deborah was complaining about pain in her lower back. I asked if she wanted to go to the Emergency Room and she said "no." She told me she thought the pain might be a kidney infection and if it kept hurting we would go see her doctor Monday morning. We went to sleep and about seven a.m. I awoke to her shaking my shoulder. Her water had broken and the bed was soaked. As I grabbed the phone to dial 911, below her nightgown I could see the head of the baby. Paramedics arrived within moments and told me to follow in my car behind them. She gave birth to a seven-pound male infant in the ambulance.

Once at Presbyterian Hospital they told us the baby had to be taken to Vanderbilt because his lungs were underdeveloped. I spent the entire day rushing from one hospital to the other. My last trip to Vanderbilt, approximately twelve hours from the time it all started, the doctor told me our newborn boy was not going to make it. She looked me seriously in the eye and, with great compassion, asked if I wanted to hold him. Again I write to you with tears running down my face. I held him for only a few minutes when his heart stopped beating. I have no way of putting into words how I felt. I held him my son Brandon Devon Humphries as he drew his last breath. I remember hearing the whirr of the medical equipment. The moment seemed to be suspended forever. It was though a part of me died with him.

* * *

Psalm 23 The Lord is My Shepherd

The Lord is my shepherd, I shall not want;

He makes me lie down in green pastures.

He leads me beside still waters;

He restores my soul.

He leads me in paths of righteousness for His name's sake.

Even though I walk through the valley of the shadow of death,

I fear no evil; for You are with me; Your rod and Your staff,

they comfort me. Surely goodness and mercy shall follow me

all the days of my life; and I shall dwell

in the house of the Lord forever.

* * *

Losing my son was the most difficult experience of my life. I knew my only hope was to rely on my faith and console my wife at the same time. We were both distraught because on top of this, the past year of our marriage had been very tough. We managed to hold things together long enough to deal with the death of our baby boy. All our experiences in this world have a place and death is part of life after all. Although a child's death is undeniably tragic, in the end we must find a way to accept God's will. As the great poet of the Bible says,

to every thing there is a season,

A time for every purpose under heaven.

A time to weep, and a time to laugh.

A time to mourn, and a time to dance.

–Ecclesiastes, 3:1,4

And the gentle girl/child, Saint Theresa of Avila, accepted her own illness with grace and wisdom beyond her years. "Let nothing disturb thee, Let nothing affraight thee, All things are passing, God changeth never."

* * *

I continued singing with The Southmen. We were kept very busy with my involvement in various concert promotions. Perhaps staying preoccupied was a way of coping with the sorrows of that time. Anyone watching my life would have said that things were perfect. They were far from perfect. I was not happy in the marriage or singing. I believe it is my choice to be happy or not. Being very unhappy with everything, I decided in the spring of 1980 to end the marriage and walk away from my career in gospel music. Psychologists would say this was the beginning of a period they call The Dark Night of the Soul, when you enter a time of not knowing the answers, wandering somewhat, which is exactly what I did!)

Even though there were times of uncertainty, there was a mystical feeling of change and new experiences to follow. Thanks to my Mother, I kept the faith believing that everything would be ok. Again thank you Mother for all your prayers. I'm starting to understand now why you worried so much.

THANK YOU GOSPEL MUSIC, IT'S ALL GOOD . . .

Chapter 6

Changes in Attitudes, Changes in Latitudes

My sister Sherril and ex-brother-in-law had an appliance business in Tulsa, Oklahoma, and offered me a position in the business. From Nashville I moved to Tulsa. I went from selling records to selling refrigerators, washers and dryers, but it didn't dampen my inner music of enthusiasm. This was the summer of 1980. The business was going very well. Tulsa was blowing (that's Southern for "booming") and going great guns. The economy was strong in Tulsa with one of the lowest rates of unemployment in the country. My family was sharing in this boom and riding its waves was very exciting for me.

I've never been one to sit back and watch everyone else have all the fun. So I took advantage of this new experience, jumped right in and made new friends, and enjoyed different activities, road trips on the week-ends to nearby cities and art festivals, food and wine festivals. My ex-brother in law liked to go to Las Vegas and horse tracks, which was a new experience for me. You might ask what about gospel music? At that time I was so burnt out that I really was glad to be doing something else. I had been basically living on the road and hadn't had much of a home life. It was a nice change to be able to sleep in my own bed for two nights in a row. Now that it's thirty years later my love for gospel music has returned. I enjoy listening to Martha Munizzi and Hillsong Worship. I was living it up, maybe a little too much but remember that Mother back in Louisiana praying for her son everyday. Jimmy Buffet wrote a song titled "Bank of Bad Habits." I think I found the ATM card for that bank of bad habits. I found myself indulging a bit too much in a party scene.

It was some time during this period that my mother had a fender bender and the doctor in Louisiana said she needed to have back surgery and that began a cycle of difficulties for her in the years to come. Other specialists came to the conclusion afterwards that too much was done during the first surgery. Over the next fifteen years or so this mistake led to multiple back and neck surgeries.

While writing this book, I just called my sister to make sure I was fairly accurate as to when Mother had her first surgery. When she answered I heard a lot of noise in the background. She just reminded me that the family was in Las Vegas celebrating her youngest son's birthday. Sorry to get ahead of my story here but I was just reminded about how wonderful my family is while writing about them. IT'S ALL GOOD . . . when you have the family I am so blessed to have.

I will never forget the experiences of the summer of 1980. The parties every night, celebrating our successful sales, the festivals we organized to raise money for charities. I made so many new friends and I admit that

I in many ways I abused my freedom but I know now that God was watching over me the whole time. When I think back on some of the crazy things I did and some of the circumstances I found myself in, I probably should have died at least a couple of times. But there's a reason I made it and now I know why. I had a destiny ahead of me; I was to be used in the future to help other people in many ways.

Tulsa was a lot of fun and I was also sharpening my skills in sales and business. Managing my sister's family business allowed me the opportunity to learn more about public speaking, positive thinking and motivational techniques in order to be successful. I became an avid reader of self-help books. I couldn't get enough information, reading book after book.

After a couple of years in Tulsa, I decided to be a gypsy for a while. I bounced all over the country but before I began hopping around, I moved back to Alexandria to spend some time with my mother. It was 1982 by now, and I decided to get into the car business. I started selling cars at a Pontiac dealership in Alexandria. I did very well selling cars and had a great working relationship with my sales manager. After being there for about three months, one day he called me into his office when I'd just completed closing a sale.

I thought I must have done something wrong. When I sat down his face broke into a big smile and he asked, "Mike, do you want to know why you are so good at selling cars?" I told him that I liked people; I liked cars and really didn't see anything that difficult in selling cars. He said the reason I was doing so well was because I was a good actor and went on to explain that I made sure that I was making the whole transaction comfortable and pleasant for the customer. I have often thought back on what he told me that day. It makes sense because regardless of what you are selling, people appreciate personality, enthusiasm, professionalism and a degree of entertainment that pleases them. Thank you Charles Walker, and you're one of the reasons that IT'S ALL GOOD . . .

In that era of my life it was as though I had ants in my pants. I needed to move on to new places and new experiences. Knowing how to sell cars made it very easy to move any place I wanted to. I could always get a job my first day in a new town with a new demo to drive. At most any dealership where I took a job, within a month, I would become a top producer.

I bounced around the country like a check with no money to back it. Dallas, Houston, New Orleans, Birmingham, Atlanta and Las Vegas were my playgrounds. I thought at one point I was ready to settle down, so I went back to Alexandria and had no trouble taking my old job back.

My mother was so happy to have me back home but by this time her back was giving her a lot of trouble. It seemed like she was having one surgery right after another one. The whole situation started to take a toll on her overall health. I thought she was still too young to have so many health problems.

Meanwhile, I started singing again and put together a group. For a time I was singing every weekend while selling cars during the week. Although I was starting to reconnect with my gospel music background, I couldn't reconnect with my previous passion. My mother was addicted to pain pills and seeing her this way was tearing me up inside. It was starting to affect my relationship with her. On a day to day basis, she was not the same mother I knew. And when I couldn't take it anymore, I decided to move to Dallas. I would still be close enough to Alexandria to be able to go there on weekends every once in a while and yet I would not be there daily. I couldn't do anything about her abusing the pain pills and it was so terribly depressing for me. She wasn't open to the help the family suggested, like pain clinics and alternative medicine.

Dallas was very good to me. I had a lot of friends whom I met in the summer of 1980 who had moved there from Tulsa because it was the next largest city.

My sister's, second husband Lindell, my sister's youngest son, James, and his wife Sherry, all ended up in Dallas too. His older brother Kenny works with him and is a major player in the success. James, I want you and Sherrie to know how proud of you I am and what an inspiration you have been in my life. Kenny, you're a whole chapter on your own. It's an understatement to say I am truly blessed to have, and to have had, the best family ever.

IT'S ALL GOOD . . .

* * *

My Mother was due for another surgery. Her surgeon was in New Orleans. I decided to go to Alexandria and take her to New Orleans. Joe was battling dementia and was in a nursing facility at the time. My youngest brother, Bobby, lived in LaPlace about twenty miles from New Orleans. We spent the night with him and drove into New Orleans about five a.m. the following morning.

For me this whole ordeal was very stressful because I loved Joe and my Mother so much and to see each of them like this was a heart breaker. They asked me to step out of the room for a few minutes during her post op. The next thing I knew there were nurses all around me asking if I was ok. I also remember my Mother's voice hollering "What's wrong?" Suddenly the room was spinning and a black shade came down over my eyes. I fainted. I let the stress get to me to the point that my body shut down.

Mother made it through that surgery just fine and was released in three days. I drove us back to Alexandria and spent a couple of days with her until my sister could come down. After each operation, the doctors would always warn us that she might never walk again, but she was determined and always beat the odds. As I said, she was a fighter and had strong faith.

Euripides the ancient Greek playwright wrote "To persevere, is trusting in what hopes he has, is courage in a man. The coward despairs."

And George Cukor said "When it goes wrong, you feel like cutting your throat, but you go on. You don't let anything get you down so much that it beats you or stops you." I surround myself with these quotes so I won't forget to be strong when negative events challenge me.

I got out of the appliance business and became fifty percent partners in a faux finish business. I have a survivor's instinct and started hitting designers, builders and architects to drum up business. My partner was an extraordinary artist and I knew I had an excellent service to sell. For those of you who are unfamiliar with faux finishing, it is decorative painting, usually aging out walls, wood graining for furniture and cabinets, or trompe l'oeil murals. It took a few months of struggling but before too long we were booked three months out all the time. We had worked hard to build this business but it paid off.

My mother was again going through hell with her back and the surgeons decided to open up her back and rebuild it with a cage. We didn't know if she would survive this extreme surgery, much less if she would ever walk again. You guessed it, she made it through and yes, she was walking within a week. She was determined to keep going. It must have helped that we all tried to stay positive. Joe was home from the nursing facility when one night just as my Mother was going to bed, lightning struck the chimney and the house caught fire. My mother, relying on a walker, finally got Joe out of bed; he was also relying on a walker. Together they escaped the burning house, the flames blazing behind them as the firemen arrived. I was in Dallas and my sister and Lindell had moved back to their home in Tulsa. My brother was the closest in distance and drove to Alexandria as fast as he could. My sister assured me that she would get down there soon and take care of everything. She closed the house down, taking my mother and Joe back to Tulsa to move in with her family. Sherril and Lindell basically became their caregivers.

Just a few weeks after mother and Joe settled in, my mother started having excruciating pains so my sister rushed her to the emergency room. A team of back surgeons accessed that the cage in her back had collapsed. They recommended emergency surgery removing the collapsed cage and replacing it with hardware. We were warned that this was a very serious surgery and because of her general health, she might not survive. We all agreed to the surgery because it was her only chance. After wrapping up a couple of things in Dallas, I hit the road for Tulsa about three and half hours north. When I arrived she had already made it through surgery and was moved to intensive care for recovery.

My sister warned me before I went in that she looked very bad. When I walked to her side, I almost passed out. Tubes were everywhere, her face was drained of color. She looked like she was already dead. I took her fragile left hand and said, "Mother it's Mike, I'm here and you know how much I love you," then I told her to pray these words with me: "God I know you are watching over me and that you will pull me through this." Maybe this was selfish on my part because

I wasn't ready to let go of her yet but she slightly squeezed my hand. I knew I had to hold myself together in the event that she could hear me. The nurse said I should leave so I told her one more time, "I love you Mother more than anything." When I walked out of ICU my sister was there with open arms as I lost all control and cried on her shoulder. Thank you my sweet sister for being there for me. I can't say enough how much I love you.

For my mother, it was a long, painful recovery with extensive physical therapy but she was on her feet and walking within thirty days. Talk about persistence! I admire her courage as well.

Maybe at times you've thought that circumstances have you trapped and from where you stand, it seems as though you can't make it. Don't give up because victory may be just around the corner with surprising gifts, a treasure chest full of gold.

Rabbi Harold Kushner has written about good people confronted with difficult life challenges: "Pain is part of being alive, and we need to learn that. Pain does not last forever, nor is it necessarily unbearable, and we need to be taught that."

(Sister and Lindell)

Chapter 7

Let's Step Away

I want to break away from time patterns at this point. I want to expound on my family and lesson learned up to this point. We'll get back on the travel machine in the next chapter. I am very proud of my family.

Aside from the trauma of my father's suicide, up until my teens, my life was pretty average. Since most of us lead average lives, I hope most of you reading have been able to relate to many of my experiences. I was not born into extreme wealth or poverty but had the Great American middle class youth with the upbringing of a very loving family.

I believe life is not as complicated as we make it. I think, for the most part, life is pretty simple. One of my favorite quotes from Ralph Waldo Emerson is "To be simple is to be great." A presidential candidate once said "It's about the economy, Stupid." Now that was a simple statement that summed up the whole election. Some of the happiest people I know are not the millionaires but the people who love their family, love life, give to others and simply take one day at a time.

My grandmother, whom we called Ma, was a simple person. She and my grandfather, Peck, as we called him, never had much. He was a painter for the local union. What they did have was over fifty years of sharing their love for each other and their offspring. What they did have was an abiding belief that all their needs would be met as well as a strong faith in God and each other. I remember as a kid it seemed like the activity they looked forward to the most every week was going to church on Sunday. Peck was a deacon in the church. If I could weigh their happiness and peace of mind, it would have more substance than that of the people I knew with ten million dollar homes and eight million dollar yachts.

Remember when I spoke about my nephew Kenny and that he was a chapter in himself? Kenny was my first nephew. Born premature, he weighed only two pounds. He had to stay in an incubator for two months and his weight went down to one pound and twelve ounces. All odds were against his survival. I think I was about ten years old and I remember a nurse holding him up in the palm of her hand. He was the tiniest human thing I'd ever laid eyes on. Born with those fighting genes to survive, he beat all odds. Kenny is now forty-seven years old. As a child Kenny was active and healthy, every weekend he looked forward to going roller-skating with his friends. He has led a healthy, productive life and is a national top producer for Carrier Air Condition sales.

Just recently my sister and her two boys came down to see me with their families.

We were sitting at a sidewalk cafe in South Beach. A good friend of mind had never met them so I invited him to join us. He told me that he heard Kenny lean over with his arm around my sister and told my sister, "Mom, I just want to tell you how much I love you." This is something that I wouldn't have noticed because that's typical in my family. We have always openly displayed loved and affection. My friend was so touched by this that he almost cried. It made quite an impression on him and again reminded me of how blessed I am to have the family I have. Kenny has a stocky build and is extremely strong. His job requires that he climb up into attics of 120 degrees checking out air conditioning units. He's about to start his own A.C. business in Tulsa. He may appear tough, but oh, what a heart of gold. As my sister and Lindell get older, I will always have peace of knowing if they need anything that those two boys will be there for them. Kenny, I love you and your gentle heart doesn't go unnoticed. James, I love you and again am so proud of the life you and Sherrie have made for yourselves. David was James' first child. What can I say, David, you are very special and I love you so much. David has a quiet demeanor; he's handsome and shares a lot of personal thoughts with me. I hope I get to spend more time with all of you in the future.

My older brother Ron and his wife Linda live in LaGrange, Ga. I don't see too much of them but it doesn't mean I don't love them; I do. They have three children, DeWayne, Robert and Alyssa and I want to tell you I love them all as well.

And then there's my baby brother Bobby who well deserves his own chapter. Bobby is the same age as Kenny. I'm not so good with dates but I always knew October 14th was my baby brother's birthday. To say that I love you and am so very, very proud of you is an understatement. It is an honor to have you as my brother. Bobby is a regional Vice President of the American Cancer Society. He has been with them for eleven years. Having several family members and friends affected by this horrible disease is one of the reasons I will donate a portion of my proceeds from

this book to the American Cancer Society to help fund research for a cure.

Bobby's job requires him to travel quite a bit and he is constantly juggling his schedule in order to have a balanced family life. Bobby and Leigh make sure they spend enough time with their son Cameron to show him love. They share experiences like traveling. They are role-model parents and introduce him to many extra-curricular activities such as karate, music, and vacations to all parts of the country.

When Bobby was a young teenager, walking into his room was like walking into an Elvis museum. I remember when he was a kid and went to see Elvis in concert. Then I remember years later how impressed Bobby was when I myself was singing on the same stage as Elvis at the National Quartet Convention and the Grand Ole Opry. (Incidentally, I also went to Elvis's funeral).

Bobby was your average kid. He graduated from Alexandria Sr. High, the same school I attended in their first year. He then graduated from Louisiana Tech. His wife Leigh is one of the most amazing women on earth. She is beautiful, knows how to cook the best Cajun food, and is a career mom and wife. She is a community bank president for Wells Fargo. They broke the mold when Cameron was born. At one time they talked about a second child, but I am glad they decided against it because no sibling could compete with Cameron. I believe he was born with a smile on his face. I love you Bobby, Leigh and Cameron. Bobby and I both are Saints and University of Alabama football fans. This past year we hit the jackpot. Go Saints and Roll Tide!

* * *

I suffered from kidney stones four times. The first was while visiting my brother Ron and his wife Linda who were then living in Memphis, TN. The stone hit me in the middle of the night and I thought I was going to die. Ron picked me up, put me in the car and had me at the emergency room within minutes. Thank you for taking care of me

Ron. I am sure after our father died that you had to take care of me a lot. Once as kid I remember crying because I missed Mother because she was at work. Ron lifted me up, tossed me in the air, put me on his shoulders for a fast ride all through the house. I forgot all about missing my mother.

I have mentioned my sister a lot. I call her sister because growing up everyone called me Mikie, my sister, Sherrie, my brother Ronnie, and then of course, Bobby. Everyone refers to Sherrie as Sherril now. To me she's always going to be "Sister." She is a lot like my mother in many ways but there's only one "Sister." You show amazing love and support for your family and life everyday. During your battle with breast cancer you were stronger than anyone in the family. Every day she assured us all that she would be okay, that God was watching over her. The only thing she asked of us was that we keep her in our prayers. .

Two weeks after her surgery I flew out to give Sherril a surprise visit. I expected her to be on the frail side and perhaps complaining about pain, but the only thing she spoke about was how thankful she was for life, that she would live a long, productive life, and we should

count our blessings every day. Sherril, you now help anyone you come in contact with going through the same thing. This is one of the reasons that 10% of my profits from this book will go to organizations to fund research for a cure for Breast Cancer as well as other cancers.

When you and Lindell moved Mother and Joe into your own home after the fire in Louisiana, you both showed what you are made of. In addition to working long, hard hours in your business, you were full time caregivers for our parents who were both on walkers. Out of everything the both of you have ever done, I want to thank you from the very bottom of my heart, especially for taking good care of our parents. I knew it was stressful and sucked the energy out of you at times.

One time I was visiting while my parents were there I observed how much Sister was coping with. Sherril and Lindell were running their business out of their house. They were answering phones while changing diapers and giving medication. They were working and caring for our parents at the same time but they never missed a beat. It was though they had it all down to a science. You are each a blessing to so many people. *Ya'all are the best!*

I am sure many of you have wonderful families. There is a saying "Blood is thicker than water." Don't ever take your family for granted. Spread that love. So much of who I am today is due to all these family members. I learn from them; they learn from me. Whenever there's a challenge in my life, one of them is always there to turn to. We all contribute to one another's moral support and cry on one another's shoulders once in a while.

Harry S. Truman once said "I studied the lives of great men and great women, and I found that the men and women who got to the top were those who did the jobs they had in hand, with everything they had of energy and enthusiasm and hard work." That's the kind of people I come from.

When it comes to your family, be supportive, loving, and stand up for each one of them. If a family member has a dream, do everything you can to help them live that dream.

Eleanor Roosevelt made a strong statement that I strongly agree with. She said "When you have decided what you believe, what you feel must be done, have the courage to stand alone and be counted." If a member of your family feels strongly that they are convinced that some particular path is right for them, support them, even if you disagree. Before I moved to South Florida, my mother begged me not to go so far away. But after I did move, she constantly supported me, telling me how proud she was of me for moving an entire business to a new city. And one of my favorite quotes along this line of thinking is from the novelist Robertson Davies: "Whether you are really right or not doesn't matter, it's the belief that counts."

Chapter 8

Floridays

P.S. Thank you Jimmy

The faux finish business my associate and I started in Dallas was doing very well. We didn't have to worry about having enough work. The secret to so many business successes lies in the number of referrals. We treated people well and remembered the customer is always right. We did what we said we would do when we said we would do it. We were always on time and that alone really shocked people. Our clients referred us to everyone they knew. IT'S ALL GOOD . . .

when you don't have to worry about finances especially when you're self-employed.

We decided to take a vacation to Ft. Lauderdale, Fl. I started researching the town several weeks before the trip. I knew I was going to fall in love with it and oh, how I was right. I read there is a real tropical zone about seventy miles north, it's the only region in the mainland U.S. with a true tropical climate, between the tropic of Cancer and the tropic of Capricorn. I had had enough ice and cold weather to last me forever when I was in New England. I'd also read about this small town having more registered yachts than any city in the world and I have always loved boats and the ocean. In my research I discovered that there was extreme, international wealth in this tiny little town with a population under 200,000. I didn't tell anyone else but I was sold, signed, sealed and delivered before I got here.

Once we arrived in the Sunshine State, I became overwhelmed with the desire to relocate there. I didn't even want to go back to Dallas. Just before checking out of our hotel and heading for the airport there was a nice, little tropical downpour. I looked out the window viewing all the beautiful landscaping and palm trees blowing in the wind, sat down on the side of the bed and cried like a baby. I knew that I wanted to be here for reasons I didn't even understand myself. Because the business had been so successful in Dallas, I knew that there was a good chance that we wouldn't make the move. Yet here we were. Ft. Lauderdale had captured my soul.

As I have written previously, I try to keep life simple. I knew I wanted to live in Ft. Lauderdale; I simply had to make my case strong enough and convince my business partner. I wanted to recreate the business down in Florida. Having worked very hard to build what we had in Dallas, along with my partner having been born and raised in Texas, I had my work cut out for me. From a business point of view, it made no sense to walk away from what we had secured. But I really believed we could far exceed what we accomplished. . I made a list of all the positive things that made sense to risk the move, put on my best selling shoes and we had the conversation. Three months later, we were living in paradise.

This quotation by Robert Moorhead described my attitude exactly: "My face is set, my gait is fast, my goal is heaven, my road is narrow, my way is rough, my companions are few, my guide is reliable, my mission is clear. I cannot be bought, compromised, detoured, lured away, turned back, diluted, or delayed. I will not flinch in the face of sacrifice, hesitate in the presence of adversity, negotiate . . . at the table of the enemy, ponder at the pool of popularity, or meander in a maze of mediocrity. I won't give up, shut up, let up or slow up."

I've always been inspired by this quote every since I first came across it. It speaks to mc of setting goals and targeting what you want. Just as the Roman poet, Juvenal, pronounced: "I wish it, I command it. Let my will take the place of a reason."
IT'S ALL GOOD.

The infamous Jimmy Buffet wrote a song "I'm the son of a son of a sailor; I went out on the sea for adventure." Although I'm not the son of a son of a sailor, throughout my life I have certainly been gung ho for adventure. Encounters with these adventures and the people whose paths I've crossed have contributed to the person I am today. As I reflect back on my life I have made my share of mistakes, and of course, I continue to do so today, because we are all flawed individuals. Do I have regrets? Only when I have hurt someone else. The mistakes made have taught me valuable lessons that I've passed on to others. IT'S ALL GOOD . . .

I am a happy individual, loving life more each day. Life has taught me to move on from mistakes and not to dwell on them. Life has taught me that tomorrow may never come, but if it does, believe it will be a blessed day. No good will come to me from stressing out. As William Allen White said, "I am not afraid of tomorrow, for I have seen yesterday and I love today." And here's a quote to remember by the U.S. Congressman, Bruce Barton: "When you're through changing, you're through." This chapter is titled after Jimmy Buffet's song. I found it an appropriate title for my move to the Sunshine State.

The first couple of weeks felt like heaven. I started hitting up designers and builders to drum up business. Things were slow in the beginning and I spent a lot of time at the beach working on a nice Florida tan. Eventually small jobs started coming in. The problem was that many of the people we were dealing found it difficult paying when they were supposed to pay, and the few who paid on time gave me rubber checks. This kept going on to the point that sometimes I didn't want to take the work that was offered.

Our nest egg for the business was running out. I started thinking that about the only thing south Floriday had given me was a Coppertone tan and that I had made a huge mistake in my decision to move there. After only six months, my business partner and I decided to move back to Dallas and get things going there again. The physical move down here had been very tough. And for me giving up was even tougher. The day after I made reservations for moving everything back to Dallas, we were talking about how hard the move was and that there had to be a reason we were here. During that conversation we both decided to do whatever it took to survive and make the business a success. The lesson here is that when fear starts to creep in, it can take over. My partner took a job with a faux finishing company. I put some ads in a couple of small publications for house cleaning. I love living in a clean house and know how to keep a house spotless. I'll admit that doing this to earn money was a bit of a blow to my self-esteem. Still, within two weeks I had more jobs than I could handle.

A friend from Dallas came down to visit. We decided to go out one night to have a couple of cocktails. Jerry's Sports Bar was packed and this guy walked by and asked if it was okay to take a seat next to us. "Absolutely" I answered. We started talking and he asked what we did. I told him we had moved down from Dallas to start a faux finish business. He told us he was a designer for one of the largest interior design companies in the state of Florida and suggested I bring our portfolio by their office on Monday morning. After so many disappointments, I really didn't believe him. However, Monday morning I took our portfolio to see him. About fifteen miles west of I-95, I walked into one of the largest show-rooms I had ever been in. John looked at our portfolio, then told me he wanted to intro-duce me to Adrian, one of their top design-ers. Both of them were very impressed and said they had been looking for a good faux finish source. Before I walked out of there I was assigned three jobs to work up some bids for. We landed all three jobs and, after that, the work started flowing in. Within a month I quit cleaning and my partner quit the faux finisher he had gone to work with. We had so much work that my head was spin-ning. I recall a John Dewey quotation here: "Arriving at one goal is the starting point to another." I sincerely believe the reason this newfound business boom happened was because after giving up, we made the com-mitment to do whatever was necessary to succeed. This poem captures my sentiments significantly.

To Risk

To laugh is to risk appearing the fool.

To weep is to risk being called sentimental.

To reach out is to risk involvement.

To expose feeling is to risk showing your true self.

To place your ideas and dreams before the crowd is to risk being naive.

To love is to risk not being loved in return.

To live is to risk dying .

To hope is to risk despair.

To try is to risk failure.

But risk must be taken, because the greatest risk in life is to risk nothing.

Those who risk nothing do nothing, have nothing, are nothing, is nothing.

He may avoid suffering and sorrow, but they simply cannot learn

to feel, and change, and grow, and love, and live.

Chained by their servitude, he is a slave who has forfeited all freedom. Only people who risk are truly free . . .

–William Arthur Ward

During this period it seemed we were living in the fast lane. Many of our jobs were long projects that gave us the opportunity to get to know the clients. So many of them were multi-millionaires and swept us up into their social lives. Clients treated us as their best friends and their homes were amazing along with their fabulous, white yachts floating on sparkling inlets. We spent Monday through Friday working hard at something we both enjoyed and over the weekends we played with our millionaire friends, who treated us to experiences we had never had before. One Saturday afternoon one of the clients took us down the Intercoastal Waterway to Miami where we docked at a private yacht club. Once docked, we walked with four others to Lincoln Road to have an eighteen hundred dollar lunch. Afterwards we spent the night on the yacht. I'd never slept on a boat before. Listening to the sound of the waves lap the side of the boat was something I felt I could get used to.

I'll never forget my first Christmas in Ft. Lauderdale. While most of my friends and family were freezing their rear ends off in Dallas and Tulsa, I was kayaking in the warm ocean waters of South Florida. I couldn't wait to get out of the ocean to phone and wish them all a Merry Christmas. IT'S ALL GOOD . . . when you're in the ocean in December.

One morning after taking my three-mile walk, getting close to the front door I heard loud voices coming from my backyard. I opened the front door quickly and ran to the backyard. I couldn't believe what I was seeing, hundreds of parrots everywhere. They covered every electrical line, fence and tree and seemed to be having a reunion in my backyard. The bold colors were fabulous, yellow, blue, red and green. And the noise was so loud, I was blown away! I got my camera to capture the canvas of backyard parrots. Then I started calling people back home so they could hear the sounds the birds were making.

* * *

One of our clients had a home here and one in Las Vegas. This couple was very kind and gen-erous to us. Every time I walked into their beautiful home I felt like I was in my own house. One week-end they flew us out to Las Vegas to see Jimmy Buffet perform at The Grande. It doesn't mat-ter where I see Jimmy perform; I am always amazed. The Vegas concert had extremely high energy; it was at a different level than any of the other performances that I had attended. I danced and laughed through the entire con-cert. Thank you Fran and Tom for one of the best weekends of my life. Tom, you're great, but Fran, I remember you tossing me the keys to your new Lexus sports convertible, saying "This is your ride for the weekend." You are one of the sweetest people I have ever met. Photo Jimmy in Vegas

It seemed we could do no wrong when it came to business. The real estate market was booming in South Florida so we  were starting to buy homes, fix them up and sell them as soon as they were finished. We were working very hard and it was paying off.

I fell more in love with South Florida experiencing the tropical climate, the amazing skies, all the exotic plants, parrots, lizards, and on and on. I finally felt I had found a place to plant my feet into the earth. IT'S ALL GOOD . . . when your feet are planted in warm sand.

Chapter 9

Sunset

South Florida is an awesome place to live. From Palm Beach south to Miami, there is a vast array of activities. Amongst the diverse events that I enjoy are the restaurants, art shows, boating, concerts, and, of course, the overall climate. There is always something going on that gets my attention. Hot spots abound. You can drive to Key West in less than four hours from Ft. Lauderdale. The drive down is a great experience and Key West reminds me a lot of a miniature New Orleans.

With business going so well, I was able to get out and explore so many different places and aspects of Florida. It's a big state and there are many special cities, flora and fauna and gorgeous beaches. You would think that everything was perfect; at least I thought so. As I became more involved in the lives of extremely wealthy clients, I found myself starting to lose focus on the things that really matter. I could see myself changing from too much exposure to high-style living. I was losing my own identity in all the entertainment and toys. I started feeling depressed and knew I had to get a grip on what was really spiritually fulfilling for me. I did a good job of hiding these feelings from other people. I was usually the life of the party and no one suspected the inner turmoil I was experiencing.

It was in this stage of my life when my sister called to tell me that my stepfather, who felt like a real father, the man who raised me from childhood, Joe, had passed away. I loved Joe so much and the news of

his death was devastating. Within a day, I met everyone in Alexandria where he was to be buried at our family plot. My mother asked if I would speak at his funeral and there was no way I would say no to her. I spoke about memories I had of him from my childhood and addressed his wonderful character. His passing was a tremendous loss to me, because he was such a precious father.

I remember when I was just a kid traveling around the state performing. Joe and my mother would drive for miles and miles to see their son sing gospel music. Many times after a concert people would address him as "Mr. Humphries" and he never once corrected them. This was because he wanted it all to be about me, rather than himself. I also remember when my mother had her first back surgeries how Joe helped her so much during her recoveries. He was by her side after each surgery to wait on her and get her anything she needed, her favorite ice cream, a special book, or blanket. Joe, I know you hear me as I write these words. Thank you for your love and support raising me up. Thank you for being such a good husband to my mother. Thank you for being Joe. I love you.

* * *

When I returned back to Ft. Lauderdale after the funeral, I was even more depressed. But my mother always told me, "you do what you gotta do," and I did. The business was booming and there was no time to sit around and dwell on losing Joe or wallowing in my introspection. Every week was full of work and the weekends were packed with social events.

How could anyone with so much going his way feel discontent? Jimmy Buffet wrote a song referring to a volcano blowing and addressed the issue of "Where will I go when the volcano blows?" His answer is, "I don't know." And that was my answer to the question of how could I be so discontent. I didn't know. My feelings of depression were similar to a repressed hurricane within.

At times I felt like I was on the bad side of the storm. At other times it felt like the eye of the storm was passing over me where all is eerily calm. I think what I am trying to relate to you is there were times when I would get knocked to the ground but I would always get back up. I never lost my faith and believed that there was light at the end of the tunnel. Oh yes, don't forget that mother of mine down South on her knees praying for me the whole time. I knew that through it all I would stay as focused as possible on everything that was working in my life and that peace would return in my life. If you are battling depression, do what you think necessary to change your negative worries to positive ways of thinking and you can overcome this down cycle. Have faith, believe, and stay focused on all your blessings. We are often stronger at times than we think we are.

* * *

There were so many good times and experiences. I'll never forget while cruising the Atlantic south of Miami one Saturday afternoon, all of a sudden a dolphin surfaced from the clear blue water followed by a baby dolphin. They dove under and then came up again from under the water. The captain told us that it was a Mother dolphin teaching her baby how to swim. This image will be with me forever. IT'S ALL GOOD watching a mother dolphin teach her baby how to swim!

It seemed like my attitude was getting better. I was smart enough to pick up a good book from time to time and maintain my faith. I have my own belief system as to the power of prayer, and I know that my creator watches over me. Faith has always worked for me.

I had a nice home, car, business and social life, but things fell apart in the blink of an eye. My business partner and I decided to close the business due to a difference in opinions. At the time this put a tremendous strain on our relationship but I am glad to say that today I consider him one of my best friends. I really didn't know what career to pursue next because there was no passion driving me in any specific direction. Just as things appeared to be getting much better, I felt like the rug had been pulled out from underneath my feet.

After much thought, I decided to move back to Dallas. At least there I would be close to family. My mother was still living with my sister in Tulsa which is the nearest big city. My sister and Lindell had an interest in real estate so we decided to start buying houses that were fix-er-uppers and flipping them. After a couple of months I could certainly see that the market in Dallas was nothing like the market in South Florida.

Around this time, my sister brought my mother down from Tulsa for a big birthday party for me. Time would tell that this would be the last time I would see my mother on her own, not tethered to my sister's home and care, nor in a twenty-four hour skilled nursing facility. But our real estate dreams in Dallas were not working out so well. I decided to go back to Ft. Lauderdale where the market was still climbing off the wall. After living in Dallas only six months, I went back to paradise.

I have found that life can sometimes be like a roller coaster. You just hold your hands up in the air and enjoy the ride. As the poem says: "Life is full with its ups and downs." I have realized that many of the downs were life's way of molding me into the man I am today. We need to face our struggles head-on with belief and faith that everything happens for a reason. Looking back on the experience of moving to Dallas and then back to Ft. Lauderdale. I can see retrospectively that this was the stage where my life would really start to change for good.

I was back in South Florida for no more than two months when the real estate market crashed. Now we were looking at losing everything–the funds from my sister and Lindell along with every cent I had–and we did. Hurricane Wilma blew through driving the last nail into the coffin of the real estate business. Not knowing exactly where to turn, I knew I needed to land a commission based high-end job in sales. Since more than half the roofs in Broward County were covered in blue tarps, the roofing business seemed to be the answer. I took a job with a roofing company based out of Dallas. When I climbed up onto my first roof and almost fell through, I decided this risky business was not for me. I decided I'd rather find the right sales position where my feet would be on solid ground rather than a soft roof.

There was an ad in the paper for a sales position at a national emergency response system in an office less than a mile from where I lived. I had never had an office position or sold anything over the phone. During the interview while taking a good look at the office, on my gut instinct, I decided to take the job. My instinct was right on target. This job fit me like a glove.

I spent eleven months selling over the phone. I exceeded my financial goals and accepted a position into sales management. I bought a larger house and could see myself in an awesome state of mind. I attribute this success to *passion*. I had finally found a newborn passion for something because I knew what I was doing was helping other people. It was during this time when I found the inspiration for my steps to "Peace of Mind Everyday."

Now in my fifties, I started appreciating all the little things every day that I had taken for granted in the past. I realized that so often the simple things in life are what make life worth living. IT'S ALL GOOD when you begin to see everything without limitation through open eyes. It's too bad that it took this long for me to begin appreciating what I have right in front of me every day, but as they say, "better late than never."

Having so many conversations with numerous elderly people taught me that there's a lot to be said for a long-lived life. Listening to all that these folks had been through and all the stories they had to tell was giving me a bachelor's degree in life experience. It seems like the ones who are the healthiest are the people taking no medications. In many cases I believe that one pill leads to another pill.

The elderly that appear to be very happy are those folks who throughout all of life's ups and downs have maintained their sense of humor. On the medical questionnaire I issue as part of my job, one of the questions asks about joint problems. One day when I posed this question, a wonderful woman answered, "My only joint problems are the ones I need to stay out of." I cracked up. And I'll never forget a conversation I had with a gentleman from Austin, TX. I was confirming his order, which would usually only take about a minute to ninety seconds. I could tell by his answers that this was a special person. I asked him what he did before he retired. He replied that he was a part of the original team that invented missile warheads for submarines. He told me in detail what these missiles were capable of doing and how many were on each submarine. Come to find out, he had an idectic memory. This means he could remember everything he's ever read or seen. I spent about thirty minutes listening to him tell me all the facts. After the conversation, I certainly felt much safer living in America. He was one of the most amazing people I've ever met over the phone. He was bright, happy and seemed to be at complete peace with himself. These are only a couple of people out of the hundreds that have taught me so many lessons. My interviews were personal as well as medical, and I gained new respect for many of the elderly individuals with whom I spoke.

One lesson, for instance, has to do with the independent thinkers I found on this job. I go along with the idea that we should dream big as Mark Twain puts it: "Keep away from people who try to belittle your ambitions. Small people always do that, but the really great make you feel that you, too can become great."

I was also inspired by the many honorable people I spoke with and I promised myself I would emulate their creative thinking. "People seldom improve when they have no other model but themselves to copy." –Oliver Goldsmith

Chapter 10

Hailey

My new career was going very well but most importantly, I finally had purpose and passion returned to my life. It feels so good when you know you are making a difference in other people's lives. I have many friends who are afraid to step out of their comfort zones to follow their dreams. My hope for all of them is that at some point they pursue their own passions.

Another aspect of my new position that I liked very much was the workspace itself. The office is on an upper floor with a gorgeous view of palm trees out of its many windows. IT'S ALL GOOD working in an air-conditioned office in South Florida, especially in the summer. I also love a nice tropical downpour with palm trees blowing in the wind. Watching this scene lifts my energy. Of course, I just want to watch from inside rather than go outside and get drenched!

At any job in a large office, the more you like the people, the more you like your work. I was blessed to work with good, honest representatives who are also down-to-earth, great people. The whole team worked well together and a combination of talented, passionate reps along with the blend of good management has created a very successful office for the company. There are people from various cultures and backgrounds that I have learned from. Dealing with people from all states, regions and cities on the phone along with reps from the melting pot of various backgrounds, gave me something new everyday to add to my life.

This position opened up the door for me to meet my co-manager, someone who will be a lifetime friend. Kathleen, from the bottom of my heart, I love you. From day one of my promotion, we shared an office with our desks positioned facing one another. She has it all in terms of what she's made of; just ask her kids. I love you and appreciate you for letting me cry on your shoulders when I needed to cry. I wish you everything in life that you are so deserving of.

Given so many things to do each day left me no time to be bored. Every time I opened the door to walk into the office, I hit the ground running until, at the close of the day, I could walk downstairs, get into my little convertible and come home. Our office exceeded all expectations and it felt pretty fine being a part of what has been referred to as a "dream team."

While my life was getting back on track, my mother's health was deteriorating. Every time I would go up to see her at my sister's I could tell things were getting worse. All the surgeries and medications were wearing her down.

It's very difficult watching a loved one suffer. I have asked myself at times, why is there pain? I don't really have an answer to that question; I just accept it and move on. But I can speculate that one of the reasons for pain of any kind has something to do with personal growth. All of us have suffered cruelty, pain, envy or betrayal at one time or another. You must believe there is a reason for everything and have faith that in the end, all will be well with your soul. My sister always updated me on my mother's condition. Mother developed a staff infection in her left foot. That situation, along with her COPD, led to the decision that she be placed in a skilled nursing facility. When the move was scheduled, my brother Bobby and I decided to fly into Tulsa on the same day in hopes of lifting her spirits.

Throughout my whole life my mother would hug me tightly and end up crying any time I went to visit because she was so happy to see me. My brother and I walked into the room and I had the same feeling when I went to see her in ICU from her last surgery. But she had aged rapidly and barely responded to seeing us. After spending less than half an hour in her room, I told them I needed to go outside to call my office. I ran out of the building and broke down. After slowly regaining control of my emotions, I called Kathleen because I knew just hearing her voice would get me through this visit. Afterwards, I went back into the room and continued trying to have a conversation with my very ill mother. To see the mother who had tickled my feet as a child in this condition was heartbreaking. On my flight back to Ft. Lauderdale, I remember all the times when doctors would tell us that the odds were against her and she would prove them wrong. There was a part of me that kept saying she would fight her way back. She had always had such a strong sprit to beat the odds.

There are times when only a mother's love

Can understand our tears,

Can sooth our disappointments

And calm all our fears.

There are times when only a Mother's love

Can share the joy we feel

When something we've dreamed about

Quite suddenly is real.

There are times that only a Mother's faith

Can help us on life's way

And inspire in us the confidence

We need from day to day.

I returned home and focused on work, praying that this eighty-two year old world champion of recovery might rally one more time.

The staff infection started spreading through her body. Each time I called trying to speak with her, my sister would only say she was knocked out completely or I could hear her screaming in pain in the background. It hurt so much that my mother was suffering this intensely. It also hurt that my dear sister had to see her like this everyday. I was afraid my sister was going to crumble as well, but she stayed strong for my mother and the family.

I was in my office on Thursday, June 14th, 2007 when my cell phone rang. The caller I.D. read "Bobby Collier." I knew immediately when I saw his name that my Mother was gone. He was on the way with his family to take a vacation and his first words were "Mother's gone." At that moment Kathleen walked into our office. Without saying a word, I reached for her, the tears running down my face. I didn't have to say anything; she knew what had happened. I grabbed a couple of things and ran out of the office.

I flew to Louisiana the next morning. The undertakers were preparing for my Mother's body in Oklahoma so I was the first to arrive. My mother loved flowers so I went to the florist to pick out the casket spray before checking into the hotel where we would all be staying. Once checked in, I stayed alone in the room until the following day as the rest of the family arrived. This allowed me time to grieve so that I could be strong for my sister. I cried, out of control, for hours. My sister had already been through so much and I needed to let out my emotions before she got there.

My sister told me that Mother had an angel with her the last few days she was alive. My sister could not see her but my mother described her in detail. Her name was Hailey. She had red hair, blue eyes and a smooth, fair complexion. The day before she passed away Mother told my sister that Christ was at the foot of her bed. I realized later that my mother had this fighting spirit to survive and she needed this angel to help her let go and cross over into eternity. Thank you God for sending Hailey to my Mother.

Psalm 121

1. I will lift up mine eyes unto the hills from whence cometh my help.

2. My help cometh from the Lord, which made heaven and earth.

3. He will not suffer thy foot to be moved; he that keepeth thee will not slumber.

4. Behold, he that keepeth Israel shall neither slumber or sleep.

5. The Lord is thy keeper; the Lord is thy shade upon the right hand.

6. The sun shall not smite thee by day nor the moon by night.

7. The Lord shall preserve thee from all evil; he shall preserve thy soul.

8. The Lord shall preserve thy going out and thy coming in from this time forth, and even for evermore.

Thank you Mother for the way you raised me up. You instilled in my heart that I should never lose my faith. You raised me up in a manner that I should always be my very best and give to others. You raised me up to believe in myself and to believe in God. You were a very loving Mother and friend. You sacrificed so much for me and all your children. No one could ever ask for a better mother . One of the songs I recorded that was my mother's favorite is titled "Because He Lives." It is so much because of you my dear Mother, that I know he lives.

* * *

Once back in Ft Lauderdale I found peace knowing she was no longer in pain even though I missed her tremendously. The grief of losing her was not nearly as bad as I thought it would be because I realized her passing was the best thing for her and I know now that I have another angel watching over me. My expectations of severe grief did not take place because of the peace I found in her passing into eternity. This is a good example of how something turns out to be much less worse than what was expected. One of my favorite quotations from Mark Twain sums up this situation: "I am an old man and have known a great many troubles, but most them never happened."

I started evaluating my mother's life as well as my own. My mother had a good life blessed with many people who loved her. She was a powerful woman with faith and talents. Although she had a great life it seemed she would always find something to worry about. Of course much of the worry was family related but not limited to that. I realized I was repeating the same pattern and decided at that point to find a solution to all this worry. It was time for me to find my own recipe to do away with worry.

"Worry affects the circulation, the heart, the glands, the whole nervous system and profoundly affects the health. You have never known a man who died from overwork, but who died from doubt." –Dr. Charles W. Mayo, M.D. And Krishnamurti knew the toll worry takes. "If your eyes are blinded with your worries, you cannot see the beauty of the sunset."

I realized for the first time in my life that worry was robbing me of "Peace of Mind." Out of all the things in my life that are so awesome, it finally hit me that I was missing out on the most important, "Peace of Mind." It was then that I made the decision to write this book *IT'S ALL GOOD . . .*

I thank every one of you who are reading my story, and my book. IT'S ALL GOOD . . . Look deep inside your own life. Do you worry in excess and if so, what and how does this worry bring good into your life?

Put on your seat belts and make the commitment to do away with anything in your life that is not allowing you to achieve "Peace of Mind" everyday.

Then you will shout to the world with me . . . IT'S ALL GOOD . . . !!

Chapter 11

Rain On Me

You make choices everyday. You decide what you're going to wear each day. I f you choose to eat eggs you can have them scrambled or sunny-side up. Everyday comes with many decisions. Many times we face choices that are good for us or bad for us. I am fifty-six years old and have heard the clichéd statements like "You can't teach an old dog new tricks, or "If you can't beat 'em, join em." I strongly disagree with these adages. My remark to these dictums is that I may be fifty-six but I learn new tricks everyday. And in regards to not being able to beat them, I am a strong soldier, capable of winning the battles I face if I have the passion to do so.

Let me ask you a question. For the most part, do you make good choices everyday or do you think you make more bad choices? Do you make most choices yourself or does someone else make most of your choices? I'm not here to judge anyone so it doesn't matter what your answers are. I just want to create one of those small mental earthquakes to motivate you into thinking more about the choices you make everyday. The well-known motivational speaker Zig Zigler, has said, "Happiness and success are not a matter of chance but choice."

Returning home from Louisiana I found I had to readjust my thought process. I had always had my mother to turn to and always knew that she was praying for me. But I realized that she is still there for me.

I think a turning point in my life was recognizing the worry factor and taking action to do something about it. By making the choice to have far less worry in my life, I found myself winning more battles and generally being happier each day. I started the process of weeding out the people in my life that were bringing me negativity. My job had so many challenges that formerly caused me worries and I started relying more on my faith to relieve a great deal of the stress. As I exercised my faith more everyday, I could see my quality of life enhanced more and more. Going through this process allowed me to understand and enjoy all the gifts that come with peace of mind such as giving, sharing, and suddenly noticing how abundant my life really is. My passion to live life to it's fullest and to give to others all the good I was capable of giving, made less room for me to give into worrying. I started feeling more peaceful with each new day. The more peace I had, the more I found myself enjoying and loving all the simple things in life. I found myself amazed at the beauty of plants, trees, skies, the moon and the stars that, in the past, had had little effect on me.

The business I was in exposed me to so many people younger than I am who are confined to wheelchairs, have no sight, or are missing limbs, and/or rely on oxygen to breathe. This showed me just how many blessings I have and how fortunate my loved ones are.

I mentioned earlier how much I liked Key West. One weekend I went down to the Keys with some friends. We decided to rent scooters to tour the island. I'm not sure how it happened but I managed to get separated from all the others. Suddenly one of those typical tropical downpours blew in and, in the heavy rain, my scooter kept stalling out. I was stuck on some part of the island that I didn't recognize at all. The rain was coming down in sheets and my scooter wouldn't start at all. It seemed like everyone I asked gave me different directions. Remember how I said I loved watching the Florida tropical downpours from inside my office but didn't really want be outside exposed to them? But this time I found myself participating on center stage and rather than fear or worry the whole situation struck me as funny. I wish someone could have taken my picture as I laughed the whole way as I pushed the scooter back to Scooter Hell. You're right again Jimmy,

"There's a little bit of fruitcake left in every-one of us."

Back at work the following week, just the thought of this experience would come to mind and I couldn't help but burst out laughing. Everyone in the office thought I was crazy. Someone would ask what in the heck are you laughing about? My reply was, I think it's just one of those things where you just had to be there.

I found myself in a similar situation one day quite some time after that. The lease was up on the car I was driving and I decided to fly to Dallas to buy a car that I wanted. It was also a good excuse to see my family. My sister came down from Dallas so we could all be together. One of my friends had never been to Dallas or New Orleans and decided to make the trip with me.

Once we left Dallas we started out on the road trip back to Ft. Lauderdale in my new car. My very good friend, Peter Hall, lives in New Orleans so our first stop was at his home. The second day there we decided to take the streetcar down to the French Quarter. Visiting with another friend, Lisa Thompson, who is the sales manager of the Monteleone Hotel in the Quarter, we walked the sidewalks for awhile and did a little bit of shopping. We were getting tired so we jumped on the streetcar and headed back to Peter's house, which is about five blocks from St. Charles where the streetcar runs. Just as we hopped off, the bottom of the sky dropped out releasing bucketfuls of rain. Our feet hit the ground the moment the downpour began. There we were with all our shopping bags running through puddles, getting totally drenched. Once we made it back to his house what do you think I did? I sat on his porch laughing out of control. My friend, however, didn't think it was too funny. I realized circumstances that I used to consider disastrous are now merely another experience for me. Why cry when you can laugh?

Quite some time after that experience I was to be challenged again. I was at work one day when my sister called me to let me know she felt a lump in one of her breasts.

When the test results came back she was diagnosed with breast cancer. I was devastated at the possibility of losing my sister. My sister is more than just a sister. She is one of my best friends, always there to support me when I need a hand to hold onto. I decided I wouldn't allow any negative fears to creep in but chose to believe she would be fine. Sherril decided to have the breast removed and afterwards she was completely cancer free. Now that she is a breast cancer survivor, she helps anyone she can who is faced with the same disease. She appears to have inherited my mother's faith and strong will. Sister, you are one of my heroes. You are a blessing and inspiration to me. Thank you for all your love and support. It is an honor to have a sister like you. I know all individuals are flawed but I must tell you once again that there is no better sister, mother, or wife on this earth.

As I continued on my path determined to worry less, seeking out the down pouring of all good things, I found myself reacting differently in so many situations. I was definitely making a conscious effort to bring continuous peace into my life, but I had a lot of fine-tuning to do. Still, to this very day, I must stay aware of each of my thoughts to keep improving my state of mind. The great Roman orator Marcus Aurelius said "The first rule is to keep an untroubled spirit. The second is to look things in the face and know them for what they are." And there is certainly a lot of truth in Paula A. Bendry's words: "If you do not find peace in yourself, you will never find it anywhere else."

IT'S ALL GOOD . . . when you're blowing off your worries, replacing them with positive thinking.

Chapter 12

Shall We Dance

I tell people all the time that music is my best friend. I enjoy music of all kinds. What I like so much about Jimmy Buffet is that most of his songs tell a story of a life experience. I like Aretha Franklin and Patti Labelle because they stir me emotionally. I enjoy Bette Midler because her voice is so smooth and has a soothing affect on me. Gospel music moves me spiritually. To me, music is more than just entertainment, it is a part of who I am. This book is about my life and I ask you to dance with me looking at my experiences and lessons learned.

Focus on all the positive things and positive reiteration. Once we have done this I am going to take you through some mental exercises that have worked for me in achieving "Peace of Mind." Keep in mind that you must have the burning desire to reprogram your thoughts and prepare yourself in order for this system to work. You must also keep an open mind. Let's dance!

I had confident expectations that this book would enhance and improve the lives of many people. I was confident that it would be successful. Before being published, the book is already a success in that writing it has made me stronger and more balanced in maintaining my "Peace of Mind." I always believed the book would help other people but never realized the effect it would have on my own life. Many of the episodes I've described here stirred up old feelings in me and to relive them was very painful. The good news is that the pain helped me resolve and seal away certain issues. The act of writing the book has worked as a unique form of therapy for my soul.

When I had to think back to when my father took his life, I learned to believe there are different lessons for different people. That incident was half a century ago and I believe there is more help for people today that are contemplating suicide. If anyone reading this book has ever had thoughts about taking his or her life, these days there are groups and people that love you to turn to. Life is a precious gift and you should never underestimate the value of your life. We are all unique individuals with something to contribute.

Another favorite quotation I came across is from Marltbie D. Babcock who wrote "Be on the outlook for mercies. The more we look for them, the more of them we will see. Better to lose count while naming your blessings than to lose your blessings to counting your troubles." And the amazing Helen Keller, who was both blind and deaf, had the inner strength and depth within her to state, "Everything has its wonders, even darkness and silence, and I learn, whatever state I may be in, therein to be content."

Remember when I wrote about the move from Alabama to Louisiana was much easier for me than it was for my mother? I believe the difference in our acclimation to a new life was due to my being a kid. Therefore I think it's important that we always keep in touch with the kid within us. I have always adapted to change very easily. In general I believe it's harder for adults than it is for children when change is necessary. As we get older we tend to complicate things more. It doesn't have to be that way. Remember to be simple is to be great. I agree with Bruce Barton who said, "When you're through changing, you're through." And the great German author Johann Von Goethe stated "Life belongs to the living, and he who lives must be prepared for changes." The truth is change is constant. I like to quote John Dewey to emphasize this point. "Arriving at one goal is the starting point to another."

As I persisted in my childhood to follow my passion for gospel music–look where that passion and persistence finally gave me! Recording my first solo album at twelve and traveling with a professional group at sixteen was quite an accomplishment for a kid living in a cotton field across the road from a bayou. This happened as a result of my believing in myself and avoiding discouragement to the point where I would give up my dream. There were times I bumped into some roadblocks, but I was always focused on the solution rather than the problem. I knew I could sing and make myself, and others happy with my singing. I knew I could deepen people's faith by showing my passion for Gospel music. "Doubt who you will, but never doubt yourself" is a quote by Christian Bovee that I feel is good advice for us all. And the great American thinker Ralph Waldo Emerson inspired me with this thought: "Self-trust is the first secret of success."

Remember the definition of passion that I like the most is "boundless enthusiasm." When I look back on what I accomplished as a kid, I was about as boundless as they come. My enthusiasm shone like a star. I don't care how old you are or what the odds are against you, with boundless enthusiasm and faith behind you, you can achieve anything. And of course, IT'S ALL GOOD . . . when you achieve your dreams.

When I fell in love with Ft. Lauderdale I was *determined* to live here. Remember the struggle with the business and almost giving up? Determination and commitment allowed me to remain in Florida and have the experience of a very successful business.

After dissolving the business partnership and returning to Ft. Lauderdale thinking that real estate would be my claim to fortune, I fell on my butt. I didn't know what I was going to do. At that time, the most important ingredient I was missing was passion. My only passion at the time was to pay all the debt incurred and keep a roof over my head. I lacked passion but kept the faith that God would open up the right doors. Remember when one door closes, another door opens. I certainly was on an emotional roller coaster during this period.

One turn in the ride was experiencing my first hurricane, a devastating storm named Wilma. The only Wilma I'd ever known was in the Flintstones! But this Wilma was no cartoon. This was the first direct hit on Broward County in over forty years. The house I was living in did not have hurricane windows or shutters. I had my first glimmer of what it takes to prepare for a hurricane by going to Home Depot, buying sheets of plywood and boarding up the house. It will suit me just fine if I never have to do that again. (My current home does have hurricane panels so now I'm good to go.)

Wilma was unusual in that she hit us from the rear, having already gone into the Gulf, she took an unexpected turn back to the East coast of Florida. I learned a lot about storms through this experience and the accuracy of the National Hurricane Center. We only had three days to prepare and make the decision to leave or ride it out. I decided to stay but believe if a storm like this ever happens to head toward Ft. Lauderdale again, I will evacuate. It was no fun with winds in excess of 100 mph blowing over for more than five hours. The noise was deafening. I couldn't see outside because of the boarded windows, but when my brother-in-law called and told me the eye was about to pass over, I cracked the door and went outside. Every tree and bush was torn and scattered; debris was everywhere. When the storm kicked in again, I was afraid I wouldn't be able to get back in. Once the eye had passed, the winds kicked back in at 150 mph and I told my brother-in-law that I thought we were going to lose the roof because the attic's insulation was blowing through all the air conditioner vents. The house was shaking in its foundation but luckily the roof stayed in place.

Despite the mass destruction, IT'S ALL GOOD . . . once a storm like Wilma moves out. This hurricane hit on October 24th, just a few weeks after Katrina bore down on New Orleans. Once Wilma had blown through, a cold front followed and without power for two weeks, it was chilly. The problem is that I'm a clean freak so after two days I headed to a hotel in Orlando for a hot shower and stayed there until the power was restored.

* * *

Still, not knowing what I was going to do for a living, I remembered Bill Clinton's campaign slogan "Keep Hope Alive." For those of you who might be politically impaired, Hope, Arkansas is President Clinton's hometown.

I was in hot pursuit of a job in order to pay all my bills and I did so. I made my six figure income in less than a year and then was promoted. This success came as a result of persistence and faith. And ultimately, the job of helping others who are less fortunate than me was what brought passion back into my life. There have been so many times in my life when I was unsure of where I might land when life throws one of those curve balls. The one thing I know now is that I will always land on my feet.

As we prepare for the steps to happiness in the final chapter of IT'S ALL GOOD, my prayers are that you grow stronger with me and find "Peace of Mind" easier to reach and maintain.

I have danced with you on the ballroom floor and at times poured my soul out to you. My intent and passion is to make others reach for the stars and sustain a peace beyond understanding for you to share with others everyday. Success is not about wealth, but about inner happiness. As L. Thomas Holdcroft says, "There may be those on earth who dress better or eat better, but those who enjoy the peace of God sleep better." IT'S ALL GOOD . . . when the mind is beyond worry.

Chapter 13

Solidify "Peace of Mind"

When you go out to a nice restaurant to celebrate your best friend's birthday or participate in the wedding of one of your loved ones I bet you take extra time getting ready. Sometimes we put a lot of effort in preparing for an event.

To have "Peace of Mind" everyday requires effort, preparation, love, faith, forgiveness and sharing. Faced with tough challenges, I remember my mother saying "there'd be days like this." I also remember an old saying, "It ain't over till the fat lady sings." I have days when I feel I am taking the role of the fat lady. I am determined to sing out to the world before the day ends that "All is well with my soul."

I'm sure everyone reading this book has faced many challenges and heart-breaking experiences. Keep in mind that this book is a summary of my life. For me to go into every detail is not realistic. I would be writing for years and the book would be never ending. I have shared some of life's battle's, not all of my battles. I have cried tears of joy as well as tears of grief. But all these experiences are life-shaping and molding me in my growth. With each new day we continue to grow. And IT'S ALL GOOD . . . to grow each day.

I am thankful for the life I've been given, all my success and trials and the lessons I've learned. Remember how I explained worry was robbing me of "Peace of Mind?" Out of all my issues, I felt that worry was the major player in keeping peace away. Worry accomplishes nothing and only brought me down.

For you it may be something else or a combination of things. Maybe you don't worry in excess. Perhaps you have a problem with trust, dreaming, relationship or abundance issues. "Peace of Mind" comes from a good balance of all the positive things. Take a good look at what makes you feel really good about yourself. Then look at anything in your life that brings negativity. Remember there is a solution to every problem you have. Think about possible solutions, rather than lamenting all the dimensions of the problem.

I remember years ago while bouncing all over the country like a rabbit. When I was living in New Orleans, I was broke with just a few dollars to my name. I was sitting on the sidewalk one day eating a bologna sandwich waiting for my clothes to dry in the Laundromat from Hell. Half the machines didn't work properly. I looked at my bologna sandwich, my surroundings and asked myself how much worse can it get? I immediately answered the question for myself and decided to not let it get any worse. I went on an interview the next day for an advertising company based out of Los Angeles and I was hired on the spot. I ended up breaking all sales records, and became regional sales manager over all of Louisiana and Mississippi. I focused on a solution rather than the bologna sandwich and lack of funds wasn't a problem anymore.

I keep telling people that life doesn't have to be so complicated. Sometimes the answer to a problem may be right in front of your face. It's right there but you can't see it because it's too simple. Remind yourself when a problem pops up that many times there's a very simple solution. Maybe the path to maintaining peace is simple, as long as we believe, love and forgive. Don't blow things out of proportion. Do what you enjoy doing. When you're hungry, eat; if you're thirsty, drink; dance when you feel like dancing; sing if you want to sing, and laugh when you feel like laughing.

Maybe it's time for one of those mental earthquakes or a volcanic belief eruption. I think some of the greatest things happen when we jump out of our security blanket. When we do this often times we uncover some of life's greatest treasures. Don't be afraid to risk when it comes to your passions. The marvelous painter Vincent Van Gogh, who suffered much in his life, proclaimed, "The fishermen know that the sea is danger-ous and the storm terrible but they never found these dangers sufficient reason for remaining ashore." And from the wise man, Ralph Waldo Emerson . . ."As soon as there is life, there is danger." IT'S ALL GOOD . . . to dance right into your life, let loose and let your hair down. A good example from my life is the time I jumped off the stage in that concert when the energy was so high. The crowd loved it. Don't get so comfortable that your comfort chokes the life out of you. My mother raised me to be all I can be and instilled in me that I should never sell myself short. Make sure everyday you are perform-ing to your optimal potential! Take on tough jobs that challenge your ability. Dive into them with excitement, love, faith, and joy. Miracles will happen. The future belongs to the people who believe in the beauty of their dreams and passion.

Regardless of your age, look at where you've been and in which direction you are headed. I was just looking at my yellow legal pad where I've written over fifty names of people in gospel music that had an influence in my life. Focus on all the positive things that have happened in your lifetime. If you think someone did you wrong in the past, forgive that person in full right now. Maybe you need to call or write them a letter letting them know IT'S ALL GOOD . . . when you forgive.

Well, alrighty then, are you still with me? We all have issues that need to be resolved in order to have "Peace of Mind" everyday. If there are skeletons in the closet, it's time to yank those doors open and make that closet squeaky clean. Make a commitment to fully release every negative incident that you are holding onto from your past. When you release old feelings you are going to feel stronger than ever before. Writing these words is empowering me to take on any challenge I face in the future. It's one thing to believe you are going to be happy; it's another thing to speak it into existence.

I have written about passion and how I believe it's one of the best ingredients in the recipe to fulfilling your dreams. My passion is to give all the possible tools I can give to as many people as possible in order to improve their lives. IT'S ALL GOOD . . . and it just keeps getting better and better. Fall in love with life. Let go of all envy, selfishness, self-pity, and anger. Let's go for it; let's have "Peace of Mind" everyday.

One small action you can perform, that makes it easier to have peace everyday, is just to smile. The simple act of smiling makes you feel better. Smiling doesn't cost a penny and yet it can be a treasure for you and others. Every time I smile at someone I feel positive energy. Every time someone smiles at me I feel that same energy. All of us have experienced heartbreak, fears and sorrow. During those times everything seems to be better when we just smile.

I believe so many people have been a part of my life due to the fact that I keep an open mind to learn from anyone. I put no restrictions on race, religion, politics, age or culture. Having this open state of mind allows more people in. It also allows me more opportunities to share good experiences with others. The more heroes, mentors and teachers we have in life, the more wind we have beneath our wings.

* * *

I want to share two stories that have happened to me while writing this final chapter. After telling you these events I then want to take you through twelve steps that have allowed me to have "Peace of Mind" everyday, one by one,.

I recently began my rewrite of the final chapter and as I came home on Monday Dec 13, 2010, I saw there was a U.P.S. package at my front door. It was from my sister and I knew it was some photos I had asked her to send. She also enclosed a couple of Christmas cards with gift cards for me. In this package there was a small yellow notebook with each page in my mother's handwriting. As I started flipping through the pages I burst into tears. I saw page after page of notes on peace of mind, how to be happy, how to live your life, keep a positive attitude, set goals, and the list goes on all backed by scripture from the Bible. Out of all the wonderful gifts I have received in my life, this is by far the most precious. My sister knew I was writing this book but didn't have a clue I was in my final chapter entitled "Solidify Peace of Mind". It felt as though my mother was watching over every move I make and that she sent me a miracle Christmas gift.

For example, she writes "How to live your life before death.

1. Faith
2. Live your life for your children to see how to live their life.
3. Give
4. Leave a Godly legacy

She wrote notes on how to know God's will. She referenced Colossians I: Verse 9. "For this reason we also, since the day we heard it, do not cease to pray for you, and to ask that you may be filled with the knowledge of His will, in all wisdom and spiritual understanding." She wrote that understanding

God's goodwill for us is a way to have "Peace of Mind."

She also wrote out Psalms 19: Verse 7. "The law of the Lord is perfect, converting the soul, the testimony of the Lord is sure, making wise the simple." Remember where I quoted that to be simple is to be great?

She asked the question on how to make a decision and answered with another question; does this decision honor God?

She continued page after page noting how you need to be committed and to have courage, to have unshakeable faith, be consistent, forgive and know there is a purpose for everything.

Keep raising your faith.

Keep thinking positive.

When things go wrong don't blame anyone, reward yourself because this is how we grow.

If you make a mistake, forgive yourself.

Drift in Spirituality!

Thank you Mother, for giving me the very best gift I've ever received, and as you well know, you're timing was perfect. Once again you proved to me that you always gave all your love from your heart. I can now, at this moment, feel my Mother tickling my feet. As I just finished writing these words sitting at my desk, I heard something make a noise behind me. It is a small ceramic and metal angel I have on my bookcase behind me that just fell over onto a glass heart that is the item I have looked at everyday as a reminder of my mother. And, of course, it landed face up facing me! If I ever had any doubt, she just solidified my "Peace of Mind."

The other story I want to share happened as I was finishing my first draft of this chapter. I had a close friend that had been helping me with this project from day one. This person helped me in so many ways, including establishing the web site, acquiring copyrights, and fulfilling all the details involved in writing a book for publication. We had a disagreement on an issue that I thought was irrelevant. It turned into an argument that outraged him. His anger reached the point at which I actually felt fearful and had no choice but to dial 911. Needless to say, I would get no more help from my friend while my whole project was threatened with destruction because this individual had all the passwords into my web site and my internet accounts. I never dreamed this would happen so I had really paid no attention to all the logistics of the web site and other accounts. I was to learn a very valuable lesson from this. I bet many of you are thinking ahead and think I'm about to say that I have to be more careful as to whom I trust with these important details.

I'm sorry, but if that's what you think my lesson was, you're wrong. My lesson was *learning to forgive* completely. I was so angry at that point that I personally felt I would have a problem with total forgiveness because the experience was so degrading. I knew that if I was to finish this book and write from my heart that I had to master *Forgiveness* and practice what I preached. I had already taken anything that reminded me of him out of my office area because I thought I'd get angry again if I saw a reminder. I knew I had to do something fast. I began to think about all the wonderful ways he had helped me. I brought a few photos and articles back into my office and focused on the positive aspects of that friendship. I accomplished forgiveness by placing the photos around my desk so that any direction I faced I could not avoid eye contact with his picture. Every time I see his face I make myself think of his warmth and generosity, and all the good contributions this person made to my life. I think of all the positive things done rather than the negative ending. I look at his face and pray that God will give "Peace of Mind," love, hope, dreams and faith to this individual. I sincerely forgive him fully and hope that his soul will be engulfed with peace and happiness. I always thought that I knew how to forgive but I needed this very intense and disheartening situation to happen to solidify forgiveness.

The difficulties, trials and hardships in life are all blessings, for they make us strong and teach us how to rely on ourselves.

* * *

Now the time has come to go through the steps that have worked for me in having "Peace of Mind" everyday. I hope they work for you. After we go through the steps, I am going to ask you for a twenty-one day commitment of mental exercises in achieving "Peace of Mind" everyday. I'm not living in some La-la-land, in that I realize we face many things that will hurt us and discourage us. But even during these battles we face, I believe when it comes to "Peace of Mind," you can maintain it every single day of your life.

The renowned French philosopher, Francois de Fenelon wrote, "Peace does not dwell in outward things, but within the soul; we may preserve it in the midst of the bitterest pain, if our will remains firm and submissive. Peace in this life springs from acquiescence to, not in an exemption from suffering."

Remember me telling you to follow your dreams and passions. In order to set an example, on 01-18-11 I walked away from my corporate American career to pursue my passion of becoming a best-selling author and inspirational public speaker thus for helping as many people as I possibly can in achieving peace and happiness. I am currently in Tulsa, Ok. to help launch a new family business as I proceed with all my projects, dreams, and passions.

Chapter 14

Michael Humphries Twelve-Step Program

I wish to thank Lawrence Ignaczak for linking each step to scripture.

The twenty-one day practice that will free you from worry into peace is as follows:

Step 1. **Give.** We must be willing to give to everyone all the good things we can give to help other people. Give expecting nothing in return. You could be a treasure of gold to so many people. GIVE, GIVE, GIVE!

Luke 6:38 "Give and it shall be given unto you; good measure, pressed down, and shaken together, running over, shall men give into your bosom. For with the same measure that ye mete withal it shall be measured to you again".

Step 2. **Faith**. We must believe there is a reason for everything and know that our dreams will come true. Realize that faith is the total vision of what's to come.

Hebrews 11:1 "New faith is the substance of things hoped for, the evidence of things not seen."

Step 3. **Persistence.** When you believe in something let no one or anything stand in your way. Don't quit when things go wrong. Focus on your goals and dreams and endure to the end.

James 1:3" Knowing this, that the trying of your faith faith worketh patience".

Step 4. **Love.** You need to love yourself, love everyone, love your life, and love all the little things that we have each and everyday. Love with an attitude of gratitude. I love to love.

John 4:8 "He who does not love does not know God, for God is love."

Step 5. **Find Your Passion**. You don't want to just work to pay your bills. Surely there is something you have a true passion for in life. Keep growing with boundless enthusiasm.

1 Thes. 4:1 "Finally then, brethren, we urge and exhort in the Lord Jesus that you should abound more and more, just as you received from us how you ought to walk and please God."

Step 6. **Keep an Open Mind.** Be willing to listen to other people and if they disagree with you on an issue, let them explain why they disagree. Remember we are all unique individuals with our own belief systems. Just because you think your right doesn't necessarily mean they're wrong. *Judge not that ye might not be judged.*

Matthew 7: 1,2 "Judge not that ye be not judged. For with judgement ye judge, ye shall be judged; and with what measure ye mete, it shall be measured to you again".

Step 7.   **Set Goals.** I have been a goal-set-
ter my entire life. I think one of
the most important things when
setting a goal is that you write it
in your own words and look at it
everyday. Make a committment,
set a deadline, and have a plan to
achieve your goal.

Proverbs 16:3 "Commit thy works unto the
Lord, and thy thoughts, shall be established".

Step 8. **Keep a Positive Attitude.** Regardless of all the issues you may be going through at this moment, it is critical to keep and maintain a positive mental attitude. Your attitude determines your actions. You have tools such as books and C.D.s.

1 Timothy 1:5 "Now the end of the commandement is charity out of pure heart, and of a good conscience, and of faith unfeigned".

Step 9. **Forgive.** It doesn't matter how deeply someone has hurt you. Know that in order to have "Peace of Mind" everyday you have to forgive completely. Remember just because you forgive doesn't mean necessarily that you agree with whomever you are forgiving. You do not need to see or interact with that person. You may not agree but you must forgive. If you don't forgive fully, that person is robbing you of peace each day. Pray that they be blessed with all good things.

Ephesians 4:32 "And be kind to one another, tender hearted, forgiving one another, even as God in Christ forgave you".

Step 10. Surround Yourself with Positive People. Gather friends and acquaintances who focus on all the good things in life. Perhaps you need to clean house in terms of your friends.

2 Thess. 3:2 "And that ye may be delivered from unreasonable and wicked men: For all men have not faith".

Step 11. **Speak Your Goals.** If you have a dream, a desire, or passion, speak it into existence. Tell yourself everyday. Remind yourself throughout every day that you will absolutely achieve what you want to achieve and that it's already in place. With no doubt you take ownership of this achievement and stake claims on it.

Proverbs 23:7 "For as he thinketh in his heart, so is he: Eat and drink, saith he to thee; but his heart is not with thee".

Step 12. **Don't Worry.** Yes, this was my biggest issue and yes, I still go through issues that are challenging everyday. Since this was my major skeleton, I decided to find a way to bury that casket. What I found on this journey was the only way I could make this happen was to focus everyday on steps 1-11.

Phillippians 4:6-7 "Be anxious for nothing, but in everything by prayer and supplication, with thanksgiving, let your request be known to God. And the Peace of God, which passeth all understanding, shall keep your hearts and minds through Christ Jesus."

Let me put this in another way. If you tell me that you believe Step 2 and Step 6 touch your major issues then you need to sincerely focus on all the other steps in order to master Steps 2 and 6. I believe if you read all the steps over and over that you can master each and every step in a very short period of time if you sincerely want to be the best you can be and achieve "Peace of Mind" everyday.

Reiteration; Reiteration; Reiteration! Twenty-One Days!

Now I want to challenge those of you who are really serious about having "Peace of Mind" everyday. I am not much of a morning person. Most days I get up around seven a.m. However, I feel like I'm just going through the motions until about 9 a.m. I ask you that for the next twenty-one days the first thing you do before starting your day is read my twelve steps to peace. The first thing you need to do is to write each step on an index card. Every morning read each index card one by one. Writing them in your own hand is important.

Secondly, I ask you to start telling yourself as you go through your everyday routine these same steps over and over. Be thankful that you have another day to be on this beautiful earth. *Today is going to be a good day; today is going to be a great day. I hope I can do something today that makes someone else's life better. I hope I can learn something new today that makes me a better person. Let me give in any way I can give. If something happens today which I see as a problem, I will focus on a solution to the problem, make the problem go away and keep on going. I will keep chasing my dream and let nothing stand in the way. It's a great day to be alive and it's going to be a great day.*

After twenty-one days this should start becoming a thought process where you form the habit of starting everyday the same way. Commit to make this work for you and guess what? It *will* work.

Pretty simple, right? Yes, it's pretty simple if you just make yourself do it for twenty-one days in a row regardless of what else is going on in your life.

If you're not already, start thinking about things you can do for your health so you can share your good energy and give good things to as many people as possible.

Master my twelve steps to "Peace of Mind" plan. Start every morning out with this thought process and you will shout to the whole world, along with me IT'S ALL GOOD . . . !!!

Thank you for reading my life, reading my story, and reading my book.
Yours truly,
–Michael

Michael Ray Humphries

I was born May 10, 1954 in Birmingham, Alabama. At the age of 10 my family moved to a small town in North Central Louisiana, Alexandria, which is located about 180 miles NW of New Orleans. This is where I developed a strong passion for Gospel Music and at the age of 12 recorded my first SOLO Album. Traveling on weekends I sang in concerts through out the South East and Texas. I finished my last 2 years of High School on the road with a group based in Boston Massachusetts. I wrote and performed Southern Gospel Music, ending up with my home in Nashville, TN.

At the age of 26 I decided to end my career in Gospel Music and began my career in sales. Going back as far I can remember to selling my records on the weekends seems like I've been selling something all my life.

I've learned that sometimes life throws us a "curve ball". I have gone through different stages in my life that has changed my course.

Through each phase I seemed to have learned different life lessons. My Passions have changed and at this stage of the "game of life", my passion is no doubt:

"Giving back much of what I have been blessed with."

Song Lyrics to (IT'S ALL GOOD)
Written by Michael

Verse 1:
If you're black; if you're white
If you are he; if you are she
If you can laugh and you can see
If you could Then you would IT'S ALL GOOD

Verse 2:
If you can pray; Then you can say
If you believe; You will receive
If you can live Then you can give
If you could Then you would IT'S ALL GOOD

Chorus:
IT'S ALL GOOD when we all hang out
IT'S ALL GOOD to dance, dream, and shout
IT'S ALL GOOD to say it out loud
IT'S ALL GOOD, IT'S ALL GOOD, IT'S ALL GOOD

Michael Humphries
Author/Inspirational Public Speaker/
Performer
Contact humphries.michael.r@gmail.com
www.mhpeaceofmind.com

For bookings and information call 918-527-
1250

Acknowledgements

M Mary Daum Hill, Deborah DeNicola, Junior Borges, Steve Garrison, Fernanda Naves, Fernanda Rigotto, Michael Vander Werf, Steven Jolly, Steve McSwain, Steve Allen Sprangler, Marvin LeBlanc, Heather LaCroix, Greg Yeager, Patrick Clark, Jack Menashe, Harry Hs, Ada Santiago, Donna Tyson, Createspace, Amazon. com, Facebook, A Day of Caring, A Best Air & Heat Inc., John C Young, Jeremy Stark, Barbara Weiland, Mary Beth Allysio, All Facebook friens and eachone of my blessed family, GOD, LAWRENCE IGNACZEK... You Are My Friend

Notes

Notes

Notes

Notes